The Best of

HOOK & BULLET

"If it's out there, it's in here"

Fishing falsities and hunting hoaxes from a magazine that never existed

W. HARDBARK MCLOUGHLIN

L&B

LYONS & BURFORD, PUBLISHERS

Printed in Montréal, Canada

10 9 8 7 6 5 4 3 2 1

Design by Howard P. Johnson

Library of Congress Cataloging-in-Publication Data

McLoughlin, Wayne.
    The best of Hook & Bullet : a collection of articles from the golden age to the present / W. Hardbark McLoughlin.
        p.   cm.
    ISBN 1-55821-316-3 (pbk.)
    1. Sports—Humor.   I. Title.
PN6231.S65M35   1996
818′.5407—dc20   95-51053
                                                CIP

Most of the feature articles (and some antique posters) in this book originally appeared in *Field & Stream* magazine. A few feature articles originally appeared in *Sports Afield* magazine.

"I hunt not to kill, but rather to have not played golf . . ."

—ORLANDO "SQUAWFISH" DE GASKET
Chainsaw Artist/Philosopher

ACKNOWLEDGMENTS

A work of this magnitude would not have been possible without the generous assistance and encouragement of a great many people. In particular, I wish to thank the following *Hook & Bullet* staff members and former staff members: Benjamin R. Quepps, Sir Irving J. Trotline, Mr. and Mrs. Lornette Holstein Prawk, Donald Wright, Quentin "Snag Daddy" Klondike IV, P. J. O'Rourke, Mrs. Anna Lee Bilgepuppy-Snypes, Barry Golson, Hampton "Trustfund" Blemmish III, J. Pillsbury MacDangal, Zoorepta Gillcrest-White, Fred Kesting, Naviss M. Flekk, Lady Viperinnia May Propwash, Marion M. Morrison, Dr. Adrian Stripmine Gwemp, David Petzal, Betsy Majthenyi, Nick Lyons, and Anja Schmidt. Special thanks go to Lord Reginald Fanshaw Wheelweight—Earl of Scheib—now, that man could paint!

—WHM, 1996

C O N T E N T S

PORTA-SLUM PARADE
— MOTOR CAMPING —

FEATURES

INTRODUCTION

In the summer of 1862, a young Welshman sailed for this country, leaving behind the treacherous coal mines where he had toiled as men of his family had for generations. He was a Gas Detection Specialist, but even so, something deep in his soul kept telling him there might be more to life than crawling about a sweltering tunnel, neck deep in muck, ninety hours a week, while cleaning canary cages. He could be wrong, but he had to find out. It was the American West which called out to him again and again, the lure of its vast open spaces and bright endless skies a thrilling contrast to the familiar, yet limited, palette of a coal shaft. The claustrophobic Celt who answered that call was my great, great grandfather Glyffydd "Llewthyswdwthllmh" (Junior) McLoughlin.

With an inner strength born in those faraway mines, Junior wandered that virile, untamed land for many years, using his creative skills to work first as a freelance graphic artist (specializing in cattle-brand design), then as a cactus and horse-head stenciler at Range Rags, a Wichita western-wear factory. Shortly thereafter, he used his meager savings to launch a highly successful home-fuel business marketing cleverly packaged buffalo chips under the brand name "Bison Briquettes" and later, "Kat'l Kole." Indeed, Junior McLoughlin knew he had found the golden land of opportunity.

Now an immensely wealthy man, Junior traveled the world for several years before settling in the quiet Kansas town of Squall Line, a thriving community nestled on the banks of the beautiful Supperation River. It was there, during the 1880s, that Junior married Squall Line socialite Zorelda Bovinnia Prutt (of the meatpacking Prutts). She would soon give birth to their only child, a fine, strapping lad they named Gwnyffllwdll (Orlando).

Junior McLoughlin spent the rest of his long and productive life in Squall Line, employing his formidable energies to launch a variety of businesses. Though all were overwhelmingly successful, the one which remained closest to his heart was his publishing house, Fire-in-the-Shaft Press, a labor of love in which he would eventually be joined by his son. Over the years, Fire-in-the-Shaft Press produced many specialty periodicals, however, one shone above them all. It would become the most influential outdoors magazine in America and the pride of generations of McLoughlins. Of course, I am referring to the fabled *Hook & Bullet*!

The editorial page of the premier edition, written by Great-Great-Grandfather McLoughlin, proclaimed its *raison d'etre*: "For all those who have gazed wistfully into a cheery campfire deep in the woods of beyond, then watched it engulf their tent; for those who have trembled in anticipation as their delicate dry fly drifted and lingered in the subtle eddies of a trout stream only seconds before they fell in; for those who have scanned high mountain meadows with the eager eyes of a hunter and upon seeing the magnificent elk etched against the sky, realized that the borrowed rifle was still 'back there' where Nature had called; Yes, for all those poor souls (like *you*!) who will never need a taxidermist, there is only one very special place where hunters and anglers always succeed and where guides never snicker behind their backs. Dear friends, that consecrated country lies here bounded by the covers of *Hook & Bullet*. Welcome!"

—G. "J" McLoughlin, Publisher
April 1895

◆ ◆ ◆

So it was for the sports afield in 1890 and so it is today, that when you happy nimrods embark on your outdoor life only to experience endless defeat in field and stream, you can still find solace in Glyffydd "Junior" McLoughlin's beloved "bible of the boonies"—*Hook & Bullet*.

It is my fond hope that this selection provides you some comfort—until we get your subscription . . .

—W. Hardbark McLoughlin
Publisher, *Hook & Bullet*
North Someplace, Vermont

Don't let
CONSTIPATION
make a
monkey
out of you!

ca. 1962

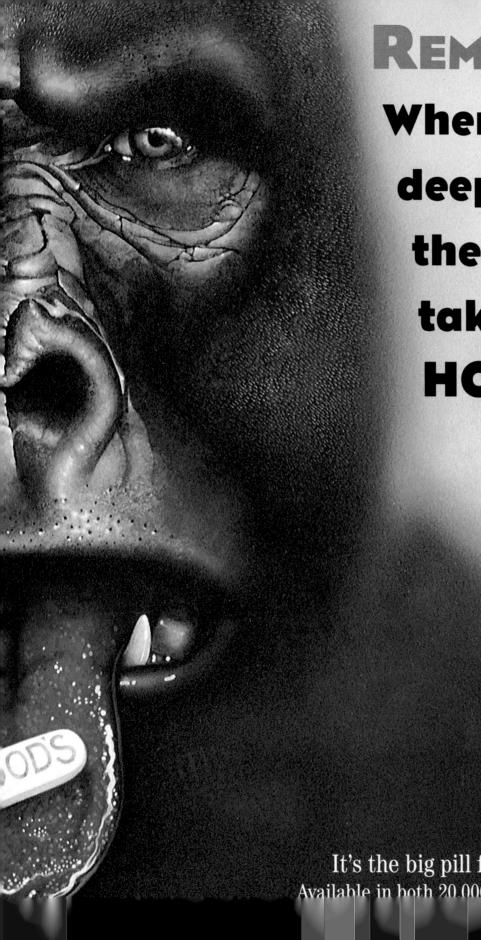

REMEMBER:

When you go deep into the woods, take along HOODS!

It's the big pill for the big problem!
Available in both 20,000- and 47,000-mg. sizes

Rumors Floating Around the Industry

Homer "Scoop" Forbish

Shown is part of a major discovery I made last year on a rundown North Dakota ranch. The bunkhouse and three outbuildings were found to contain vast quantities of motion picture equipment—cameras, editing machines, sound gear, special effects devices, and costumes from the 1930s. Local townspeople said they knew little of the ranch or its history, only that it had been abandoned for over thirty years.

MONTHS OF investigation by *Hook & Bullet* have revealed that the original owner was Tink Dopis, internationally famed hunter and fisherman. Amassing a fortune from his successful buck-lure vending machine company, he bought the ranch in 1936, and there pursued his hobby of home movies. The most elaborate of these undertakings centered on a seventy-foot papier-mâché mock-up of a German dirigible, which he named *Hindenberg*.

VERY SHORT PEOPLE were used in the close-up shots of people boarding the zeppelin. This casting technique, combined with clever use of camera angles, produced the illusion of an 800-foot-long airship! An eleven-inch model was used in the subsequent "tragedy" scene. A faded photo (unprintable) survives showing how the model was hung by wires over a tabletop landing field. Notes on the back explain that the fuselage was stuffed with cotton balls soaked in head cement thinner and set on fire. The dramatic sound effects were produced by crinkling cellophane in front of a microphone at a cattle auction.

RENTING HUNDREDS of theaters, Mr. Dopis premiered his film nationwide on May 6, 1937. It proved so convincing that audiences believed they were viewing a newsreel! That it was all fiction and that there never was a *Hindenberg* or a Lakehurst, New Jersey (the fictitious scene of the "accident"), was never grasped.

HERE IT IS 1951 and Mr. Dopis is at it again! He's been traveling about the country showing his "home movies" at various rod and gun clubs and raving about the "undiscovered" and "spectacular" trout fishing to be found in Argentina and New Zealand. Sure. No doubt his clever trick photography will con a few poor twits into going, but not me! Ten-pound browns? Eight-pound rainbows? Tierra Del Fuego? You'll never get me down there, pal. I'm no sap, I know the Battenkill when I see it.

SEE and BE SEEN

IN A 1909

The "Cape Hatteras"

$5410

The Lumino Safety Motor Car Co.
PEEVEY, KANSAS

Lumino

Note: This ad represents the only marketing effort made by the doomed Lumino Safety Car Company. Hopes for public acceptance of the machine were dashed when, after one year, none of the six cars completed had been sold. This was no doubt due to the terrifying experience prospective buyers had test-driving them. While visibility was excellent, cornering and sudden stops in the top-heavy vehicle were traumatizing.

Readers traveling through Frabial Corners, New Hampshire, will recognize the Founders' Obelisk in Spratt Park as being a cement-filled Lumino.

ca. April 1994

••••

Rumors Floating Around the Industry

FISH OF THE CENTURY!
NEW WORLD RECORD LARGEMOUTH BASS!

J. Staunton Rant

For the past sixty-two years, George Perry has held the Largemouth Bass World Record, which he set on Georgia's Ocmulgee River. Today that venerated title belongs to Panin Chakravar Sarojini, a fifty-one-year-old businessman from India, who demolished the legendary Perry mark of 22 lbs. 4 oz. with a lunker largemouth weighing in at a whopping 37 lbs. 14 oz.!

THOUGH THREATENED several times over the past two decades, Perry's record did not fall to a fish caught in Florida as predicted by the "bassin' pros." The tremendous catch was taken on live bait February 28, 1994, from a five-thousand-acre irrigation reservoir on the Sarojini rice plantation near Irinjalakuda, Kerala Province, India! It was the second of three bass caught and released that day by Mr. Sarojini. (American and Indian tourism officials were present to witness the scheduled record attempt.) Astonishingly, all three fish bettered the existing world record, with weights of 29 lbs. 2 oz., 37 lbs. 14 oz., and 30 lbs. 1 oz.!

HOW COULD A BODY of water in southwestern India contain a population of colossal bass sufficient to produce, on demand, what had been referred to as the "million dollar fish"? Says Florida's famed icthyogeneticist, Dr. John S. Rath, "In this unusual circumstance, where the resident fish display extraordinary growth, the evidence is overwhelming . . . diet!"

DR. RATH continues, "We know the reservoir was completed in 1927 and stocked that same year with a seeding of three thousand fry taken from Kingsley Lake, Florida. There was nothing exceptional about those original bass; in fact, the Sarojini trophy population began as very average bass. And no, they are not hybrids! They remain genetically pure Micropterus salmoides. They're just the biggest in the world!

THEY GOT THAT WAY thanks to a diet comprised of "Bhavali," suckers (Catostomous Atingalli) which are found *only* in the Indian rice drainages! "The locals have no use for them but I guess they are great bass food!" You can say that again, Dr. Rath!

NOW EVERYONE wants to know, "Did Mr. Sarojini catch the biggest fish in his little pond?" "No," he laughs, "each year we see them spawning, and there are many, many that are of larger size! Many, I tell you! Many! Why don't you come and try *your* luck?" You bet we will!

SO PACK YOUR "hawg sticks" and book a passage to India, bassin' guys and gals! The incredible Sarojini pond is open and so is the brand new lodge!

REMEMBER, if the new world record *is* ever broken again, there can be no doubt where that fish will come from! So, we'll see ya' there, at beautiful Sarojini Lodge—it's Bass Heaven!

To make reservations for your trip to Bass Heaven Contact SAROJINI TRAVEL Fort Lee, N.J.

Postscript (two months later):

HOOK & BULLET regrets to inform its readers that the recent special insert on the new world-record bass was an advertising "gimmick" that went a bit too far. There is *no* Sarojini Lodge. We apologize to the hundreds of families who now have a bassin' guy or gal somewhere in India. Queries regarding their whereabouts should be directed to:

the FBI
and SPAVISH, NORPTH, and HIGGINS,
Attorneys for SAROJINI TRAVEL

11

Rumors Floating Around the Industry

CASTING CARNIVAL

To the Editors at Hook & Bullet: A friend of mine at the Endless Fishing Pap Network (EFPN) got hold of these confidential memos and a printer's proof of the poster. I thought you'd be interested.

FROM: *Jo Jo Scrutts*
TO: *Gene Poole*
DATE: *2/27/95*
SUBJECT: *"Casting Carnival"*

Boss: You've probably seen the numbers on our Saturday morning bass-fishing show, and we both know this dog's heading for the Land Where Old Programs Go. We're down to two sponsors: Yank & Krank Tackle Co. (makers of Zombie Winch Reels and Uncle Jimmyz Nukular Wurmz) and we've still got Deep See Fish Finders. (By the way, the Deep See Outfit is being sued for false advertising. You remember the ad that said their product could find a ¾-pound flounder at the bottom of the Marianas Trench? I warned them.) Anyway, we have to save this tire biter, so let's put a new twist on it. We'll call it "Casting Carnival," and hype it as a "wet, wild, and wacky sixty minutes of angling antics."

The format is like this: Participants get points for gaudiest jumpsuit, silliest hat, greatest number of casts, highest combined-horsepower outboards, heaviest line test used, highest average speed maintained between designated fishing holes, most decals, etc.

Ties between these clowns would be decided by a "Rural Cliché Scream-Off." We get an applause meter right out there at dockside and have these guys yell "LAWD 'AV MUSSAY!" or "COME TO POPPA" or "THAT THERE'S A GO-RILLA!" At the end of the broadcasting season, we bring back the ten top-scoring contestants to compete in a two-hour "Laffmaster Classic." Same rules as before. The winner is "Laffmaster of the Year."

The advantage to EFPN is that this is the same stuff we're doing now. We just play it for intentional laughs. We don't spend any more money, so the beaners will love us. Let me know what you think.

FROM: *Gene Poole*
TO: *Jo Jo Scrutts*
DATE: *2/28/95*
SUBJECT: *"Casting Carnival"*

Jo Jo: I like the idea a lot, but I'm puzzled. Where does the actual fishing come in?

FROM: *Jo Jo Scrutts*
TO: *Gene Poole*
DATE: *2/28/95*
SUBJECT: *"Casting Carnival"*

Gene: You're missing the point. None of this has anything to do with real fishing. Never did. In any event, we need an answer by the end of the week. I hope you decide to go with it. I think "Casting Carnival" is a winner.

PORTA-SLUM PARADE
– MOTOR CAMPING –

GRAND CANYON EXTENSION A HOAX!

ca. 1912

♦ ♦ ♦

Rumors sweeping the nation that the United States government has been funding the construction of an additional fifty miles of Grand Canyon are false! *It is simply not true!* We at *Hook & Bullet* feel obligated to inform any readers planning a motor camping trip to view the work in progress that *it is not happening!* A spokesman for the State of Arizona said the "doctored" photographs shown to the general public were simply a ploy to boost tourism and that his state "regrets any inconvenience to individuals traveling west to view the excavations." He further added that in fact, "funds won't be available for the extension until next year. . . ."

PORTA-SLUM PARADE
— MOTOR CAMPING —

MOTOR CAMPING NEWS

January 1931

Leroy Jowsen

❖ ❖ ❖

Learn from this! Ten miles outside Snivel, Arkansas, Bert and Maude Cormorant were horror-stricken to discover smoke and fire spewing forth from this brand-new 1931 Klassy Koach. Knowing they had little if any hope of extinguishing the inferno, they sped along Highway 4 and took their blazing home-away-from-home directly to the Snivel Fire Department. Alas, it was to no avail. The conflagration spread, destroying both the eighty-year-old firehouse and the Snivel Museum of Fine Art located in an adjoining building. The entire collection was lost, including twenty-one irreplaceable works by the seventeenth-century Dutch painter Jan Ver Meer and three Fabergé eggs loaned to the museum for its show, *Poultry—It's The Art of the State.*

Visitors to the region might get some consolation by heading down the road to the nearby town of Gut Creek, home of the Flentz Lamp Wick Braiding Company. If you've ever looked at a wick and wondered, "Say, how'd they make that?" then the 3½ hour Flentz Factory tour will provide all the answers! Be sure and bring your camera!

ca. 1973
Mark Ferret
(*Hook & Bullet*
Investigator At Large)
◆ ◆ ◆

NOTE: *Hook & Bullet* readers travel far and wide in their pursuit of game, "So why not see something different along the way?" That was the sentiment of our own Mark Ferret, who spent twenty years with the magazine researching and then revealing the monumental blunders and cover-ups that state tourism bureaus never brag about. Here are the two examples that, in 1973, won him investigative journalism's highest award—The Elliot Schnauzer Golden Blindside Medal.

HOOVER DAMS
◆ ◆ ◆

THIS PHOTO is conclusive proof that the Hoover Dam was built twice. This is Hoover Dam number one. A surveyor's error (a misplaced decimal point) resulted in the dam's construction a little over one hundred miles too far to the left. Located outside the small desert community of Mesquite Spring, this enormous structure has yet to arouse curiosity. The area's inhabitants think it's a drive-in. Fearing adverse publicity, the Department of the Interior has

kept a lid on the multimillion-dollar blunder since 1935 by providing movies for the "drive-in." Showing the day this photo was taken was *High Noon* and a short feature, *The Wonderful World of Grenades*. The latter is an Army training film.

A LONE SPEAKER stand indicates the size of Mesquite Springs; the projector is placed on a card table. Ironically, electricity is supplied by a one-horsepower gasoline generator.

SEVERAL DOZEN badly damaged bulldozers, in various states of decay, were found in the vicinity. This lends credence to the theory that there was some attempt by the construction companies involved to push the dam into position on the Colorado River, 112 miles away.

THE ST. LOUIS SPACE NEEDLE
◆ ◆ ◆

OCTOBER 28, 1965—The disastrous fall of the tallest space needle ever erected is captured here in oils by an Iowa artist. (Both painter and canvas later disappeared under mysterious circumstances.)

Built to commemorate the St. Louis aerospace industry, it was christened "Pathway to the Moon," and rose to a majestic fourteen hundred feet before buckling twenty minutes after

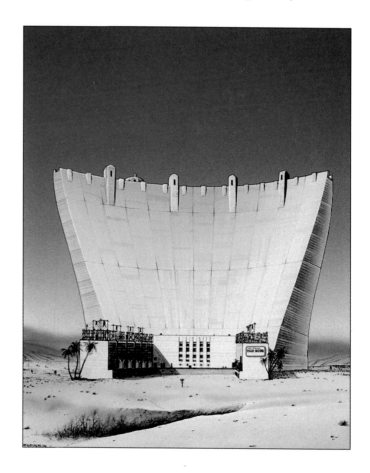

PORTA-SLUM PARADE
– MOTOR CAMPING –

its dedication. Clearly visible is the Observation Deck, which housed a gift shop, revolving restaurant, and a country and western FM station. A sophisticated drive train permitted the radio station's turntable to rotate the restaurant at 45, 33⅓, or 78 rpm, depending on the record being played. Unconfirmed reports indicate that over three hundred patrons, twenty-two busboys, six chefs, and a cashier perished as the

twirling eatery screwed itself into the Mississippi mudbank.

NUMEROUS LAWSUITS by the victims' families were thrown out of court when their lawyers found themselves unable to provide legal proof that the Space Needle had ever existed. All relevant documents had been ordered destroyed by the city council, and the structure was immediately rechristened "Gateway to the West." How-

ever, it is known that the city paid medical expenses for a number of persons maimed by an unexplained shower of Bluegrass albums.

ONLY THIS PRINT and a hot-pink "St. Louis Space Needle Souvenir Pillow," which washed up later at New Orleans, bear testimony to the ill-fated tower.

Troxel Thrumus
RV-ing Editor

◆ ◆ ◆

Krakatoa! Vesuvius! Mount Saint Helens! What's next? Mount Rushmore, that's what! You read it right friend, an' ol' Troxel's willing to bet money on it. Ol' Mount Rushmore is due east of ex–Mount Saint Helens and is located smack-dab on the Allyor Fault. Ya' don't need ta be an expert to see that rock pile's gonna go! I give it a year—max.

WANT MY ADVICE? Forget camping in South Dakota. But if you just have to see Rushmore, at least be careful! If you go there and you're suddenly overwhelmed by the stink of sulfur, and the sun is obliterated by smoke, walk slowly but deliberately to your car. Try not to attract attention. You'll just cause a panic, and the last thing *you* need is a traffic jam! Take 79 North, grab a bite in Rapid City (All the Presidents Menu is a good feed), then head upwind on I-90 West—an' start lookin' for a new campsite, pilgrim.

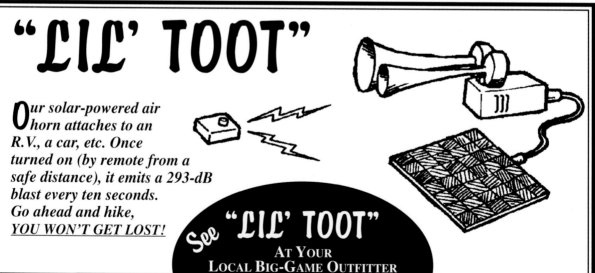

"LIL' TOOT"

Our solar-powered air horn attaches to an R.V., a car, etc. Once turned on (by remote from a safe distance), it emits a 293-dB blast every ten seconds. *Go ahead and hike,* <u>*YOU WON'T GET LOST!*</u>

See "LIL' TOOT"
AT YOUR
LOCAL BIG-GAME OUTFITTER

DROPPINGS

EDITORS: Nov. 1, 1939

I read your hunting editor's column about pinning a white rag to the back of your jacket when you're out deer hunting. I must warn everyone, I tried that 'tip' Opening Day and I was taken for a deer and nicked in the elbow by the bullet of another hunter. . . .

—**D. V.,** Blemish, Pennsylvania

DEAR D. V.:

Your warning is well heeded. Readers, learn from this! While the author of the letter fails to mention distances involved, there is nevertheless no excuse for sloppy shooting. Know your rifle and practice, practice, practice! 'Nuff said!

—**The Editors**

HOOK & BULLET: November 1, '58

You widowed me! Your hunting 'expert' recommended going after deer with a white rag pinned to the back of your jacket to fool the deer into thinking you're one of them! My husband did what you said and was bagged at dawn of Opening Day by another hunter with one shot from four hundred and fifty yards away. . . .

—**M. G. R.,** Backwash, New Hampshire

DEAR M. G. R.:

You don't mention it in your rambling four-page letter but that was some kinda shootin'! Betcha the fella that cancelled your hubby's check was usin' that great flat shootin' sizzler—the legendary .270. Are we right?

—**The Editors**

MR. HARDBARK MCLOUGHLIN: (Printed 1995)

I have been reading your column in Hook & Bullet *for years and I want you to know that I think you are the best*

in the business—no one else comes close! Your vast experience, your wealth of knowledge, and the unflagging soundness of your judgment so evident throughout your writings are the reasons I value your opinion highly. With the foregoing in mind, I come to the point of this letter—

In recent years, as we all know, the hunting and fishing media have come to be dominated by one man whose popularity continues to soar. Of course, I'm referring to Bolivar Femp! Though I remember seeing a few of his pieces back in the 70s in Poacher Life, *and* Carp, Gar, and Sucker, *these days he's everywhere! He's got a daily three-hour talk radio program; a television show; a newsletter,* Spoor; *and a hunting column, "Hair in the Scope."* Death in the Deep Stuff, *his eleven-volume autobiography, is the basis for a thirty-hour documentary funded by the NEHA (National Endowment for the Hunting Arts)! And as if that's not enough, he's signed to star in a major movie about duck hunting called* Blind Ambition! *Hell, I even saw his recipe for Graying Chili in the woman's magazine* Monthly. *It's amazing!*

Well, I've hunted and fished in many of the same places he has, and all I've ever heard about him from the lodge owners, guides, and professional hunters has been overwhelming negative! Whenever his name was mentioned, it was preceded by words like cur or lowlife!

Hardbark, those people told me horror stories! According to them, Mr. Femp was jacking deer, gill netting trout, and even stealing other hunters' racks! One outfitter said he caught him changing the zero on a fellow's rifle, and another told of Femp's refusing to leave base camp and then paying off the successful hunters to get him photographed with their game!

While he sounds like a useless sniveler who couldn't track an elephant through wet cement, none of this information matches the media image of the man or my impression of him!

You see, I met him briefly back in 1990 when my wife, Lovelda May, and I were booked at the Bear Bones Lodge up in Kodiak. I must say he was a dashing figure of a man and seemed pleasant enough. We chatted a moment and he told us he was a little under the weather and would not be hunting for several days. The next morning Lovelda May was feeling poorly and told me to go out to the line camp without her. Ironically, both of them ended up missing the entire hunt. Not me! I stayed out in the bush for ten days and finished up with a really fine Alaskan Brown that went nine feet eleven inches! Back at the lodge, Femp offered his congratulations and then asked if I would take a picture of him next to my prize. He said it would be the only bear he'd get on that trip! We all laughed. Anyway, though I only spoke with him a few minutes all told, he seemed okay to me at the time.

In fact, I remember my wife saying that he was absolutely charming.

So, Hardbark, you're an insider—you know what's going on. Is this Bolivar Femp an alright, stand-up kind of guy, or what? I sure am confused and would really appreciate your input.

Your admiring fan,
Quentin Geep

P.S. Enclosed is a picture of my four-year-old boy on the Kodiak rug. What do you think?

DROPPINGS

DEAR MR. GEEP,

I'm afraid that professional ethics do not allow me the liberty to comment on the morals of Mr. Femp, or anyone else, for that matter. However, I can say that I have seen advance copies of his autobiography and I urge you, upon its publication, not to read Chapter 7, "Fair Game—Lodge Ladies and Other Wild Women of the Wilderness." In particular, avoid the section on Alaska. You should also ignore the limerick on pages 341–343, despite the fact that Lovelda May is a very common name.

As to the photograph, since I don't know what *you* look like, I can't say anything about who your son resembles—(if that was your question). If it *wasn't* your question, then heyyyy, that's some bear, Pal!

Regards,

W. H. M.

Pot Shots

ca. 1977

Wild Game Cooking
with
LOVEENA JEAN BRIMSTONE

This is for all you fantasy "mountain men," "trappers," and "voyageurs" out there who constantly write me askin' the same question: "What's the secret to quickly recreating authentic meals of the early West?"

WELL, *"RAZORBACK JIM,"* "Pig-Iron Mike," and "Pierre le Grumman," there's a coupl'a tricks you can use! First, no matter what you're cookin' (meat, fish, poultry, or unidentified) you should always have a poke of medium-coarse sand on hand. Sprinkle it into the food according to how far you're supposed to be from the fort. Farther out—more grit! (If you're pretending to be really tough, add more—and perhaps even a dash of pea gravel.) A lot of fellows carry a poke full of ashes which they also use to "age and authenticate" canned or frozen goods. A layer over the top is all you need.

*A*NOTHER GREAT TRICK that works real well in stews and soups is a pig's ear, a six-inch square of deer hide, or if you can't lay your hands on those, just go down to your "suttler" (tackle shop) and pick up a fleece patch or two. Whatever you get, simply drop it into the boiling pot a few minutes before it's served. You just need enough time for the hairs to separate from the hide and float around.

*N*OW DON'T be afraid to use your imaginations! I mean, you're already pretending, so why not extend yourself a bit? Make believe your wagon train has been stranded for weeks in a snowy mountain pass and add a button or two! Just have fun with whatever you're fixin'— and remember, serve it either lip-searing hot or eye-hurtin' cold! But never just right!

—Bone Appyteet!

MOLINE TRACTOR PRESENTS

the 1978 D-2
"FLYING PLOWBOY"

Moline Tractor
Moline, Illinois

Around the world, bush pilots agree: "There's no dirt strip too tough for a . . . **FLYING PLOWBOY.**"

RECYCLING TIN CANS

Snevis J. Gunnul

• **Boating Editor** •

◆ ◆ ◆

"They gotta be good for somethin'," said Pacific Fleet Commander Admiral J. Armstrong Bowline after viewing the dozens of obsolete destroyers mothballed at Pearl Harbor. He was right! Six months later two of the ships were bolted together, creating the U.S. Navy's first "attack catamaran"—the USS *Oahu!*

Its sea trials were spectacular, resulting in the creation of an attack catamaran fleet numbering thirty vessels. Now fifteen years later, the crafts are being sold as surplus to civilians, thus clearing the way for the newer, state-of-the-art catamarans currently on the drawing boards.

This is a great opportunity for American charter boat operators, *so get your bids in now!* Remember, they don't build 'em like this anymore. Besides, think how many "rods" you could haul out to the kelp beds on one of these babies!

◆ ◆ ◆

OVER THE HORIZON

Lee Daiwa

◆ ◆ ◆

Next time you're annoyed at seeing another angler approaching your pool, relax. You don't know the meaning of the word crowded. Just take a look at the latest outdoor thrill from California— mass hang gliding! Giant crafts capable of carrying thirty to forty persons are just coming on the scene. Why? Just ask Cosmo Aerhed of Flock Flyers Manufacturing: "So we can share the experience, of course!" No pal, you haven't seen crowds yet. . . .

EAR-SHOTZ

NOTE: In a futile attempt at diversification, the radio and gramophone manufacturer SHOTZ AND SONS created this forerunner of today's electronic game ears. Weighting a hefty 26 pounds, the cast-iron and maple device was doomed to failure since it inevitably forced its user to stoop, thus ensuring that the only sounds ever amplified were the shuffling of his own feet and the rasp of an occasional insect.

ca. 1921

UP AHEAD
Predictions of Things to Come

ALDO REY HUXLEY

Campfire friends, as I stare into the flames, I see many things—some good, some not so good. What does the Flickering Fire to the Future show me this month?

I see, fellow trail travelers, into the year 2000! I see that African game preserves, which we currently measure at thousands of square miles, have become no larger than a shopping mall! I see genetic engineers perfecting techniques that will scale down the mighty rhino! I see people everywhere wanting the new Toy Rhinos for house pets and their popularity rivaling that of the dog. I see the cost of rhino taxidermy plummeting.

Until the next Flickering Fire to the Future,

I remain,

Aldo Rey Huxley

NOTE: The "Up Ahead" column ran in 1960 for less than six months. Huxley's final piece about alien robots kidnapping fly fishermen from the fabled trout streams of New England lost most readers.

Mr. Huxley's Future Fire was doused by the waters of reality when he was canned in the same month. He hadn't seen that coming, either.

The Ballad of J. Staunton Haye

IAN THROZZELL

Of all the men, since way back when, to fly fish for glorious trout,
There's one so sorry that I've penned his story to ensure the truth comes out.
While most fellows fish with a simple wish—just to be on a stream gives them pleasures,
This chap was cold, for as if dredging gold, he thought only of weights and of measures.

Yes, J. Staunton Haye by far and away was the most arrogant man you could see,
For he knew to the core that never before lived a fly fisherman better than he!
Brook, Rainbow, or Brown, whether upstream or down, catching trout was his only vocation,
"When it comes to the fly—there is none but I," was his typically smug declaration!

No, Haye did not jest when he bragged, "I'm the best, that o'er trout ever waved a wand!
Lads, I need but one dry and in the wink of an eye will succeed on both river and pond!

"Oh, I cast with such style, double-hauling a mile and with a presentation so soft,
That it gives one a thrill just to ogle such skill at keeping a fly line aloft!"

On the caddis and stone or mayfly he'd drone in Latin taking bilingual glee

In knowing the names (at least so he claims!) of every bug, insect, and flea!
Too bad where he'd go, he'd take that ego, with its size approaching unreal,
And command, "Hey there, fool, you may fish in this pool—after I've loaded *my* handsome creel!"

Soon all the world's anglers and fishing line danglers have heard of J. Staunton Haye,
For the man was devoted to getting promoted in every damn possible way!
Through endorsement and poster this trout-catching boaster became the fly-fishing world's hero
A legend we knew (with a false cast or two) stood a chance of failure near zero!

Well, I'm seldom vexed and rarely perplexed but I was becoming highly suspicious—
For it was Haye's own law that none ever saw the fly he would use to outfish us!
With his average so high we all wondered why divulging it caused such resistance,
But J. Staunton Haye merely waded away and kept others astream at safe distance.

So all the past season, ('twas his secret, the reason), I followed the selfish sport.
I vowed, "'Fore I die, I'll have the name of that fly, Hayes's furtiveness I shall thwart!"

I hid behind rocks, armed with just binocs, and spent all my time scrutinizing,
For my mission was clear, and I must bring no gear, even though the trout might be rising!
In streams far and wide this author did hide in waters both chilly and cold,
And for days on end watched Haye cast and mend 'till the blue of the sky turned to gold.

In the big Yellowstone this old fellow's tone got raised an octave or two
And in the Battenkill I sat until hypothermia did ensue!

On the freezing Au Sable I prayed I'd be able to solve the accursed mystery,
For all that wet stealth was making my health a thing of trout history!

Then on the Letort, where I watched Haye cavort, I saw what he'd used so discreetly,
When with the furtive look of a petty crook he opened a fly box by Wheatley!
What met my eyes were not delicate dries tied as tiny as germs,

But hidden within like some secret sin lay a half-cup of dirt . . . and some worms!

Of all the men, since way back when, to fly fish for the glorious trout,
There's one so sorry that I've penned his story to ensure the truth comes out.
While most fellows fish with a simple wish—just to be on a stream gives them pleasures,
This chap was cold, for as if dredging gold, he thought only of weights and of measures.

Powder Burns

Muzzleloader News From

OL' "GRIZZLY JOHN" LEATHERFETISH

It will still be a while before Ol' Griz' is able to report, as promised, on all the doin's at the "Ninth Annual Mountain Man Hoorah Days" out in Scabrous Flats, Wyoming. We were all looking forward to his piece, but by now readers have seen the pathetic news footage of all 2,300 of those beaded, fringed, and trichinosis-wracked souls being evacuated by chopper to the Jim Bridger Memorial Hospital in Pinedale. Had it not been for the group's satellite-linked communications center with an 8-foot dish discreetly located in a central tepee, the outcome might have been tragic. . . .

(continued) ☞

NEXT TIME GET A

BLAZ·O·

SCREW DOWN LAMP

Powder Burns

(continued)

OL' GRIZ' would like me to pass on his gratitude for all those get-well cards; he offers a special word of thanks to Col. Harvey "L. Z." Sikorsky who was up in the AWACS coordinating the 30 National Guard HUEY'S that pulled all those mountain men's partially cooked pig parts out of the fire! Says Ol' Griz' "hisself": "They was like olive drab angels of mercy come down to pluck us out o' that Valley O' Death—just like they done all them other eight years. I says: Bless em' an' may their trails be easy."

Amen to that!

—**Quentin Kevlar**
Hook & Bullet
Tech Talk Editor

TACK'L TALK

ca. 1936

Egmont J. Corrigan

◆ ◆ ◆

Regrettably there will be no more Tack'l Talk emanating from the prolific pen of our fishing companion of so many sweet years. While testing Saunders brand self-inflating, sink-proof safety waders, Egmont J. Corrigan passed away. Yes, dear readers, fate, the vandal of life, shot out his porch light this past July 17 when a malfunctioning valve mysteriously ran amok, hyperinflating his waders and exerting pressure upon him (before they exploded) equal to that at the bottom of the Mariannas Trench.

HIS STRINGER may now be empty—but we will never forget him.

HE LEAVES BEHIND his dear wife Millicent Snodgrass Corrigan. We offer our condolences and all our well wishes upon the announcement of Millicent's engagement to Lathrop Saunders of Saunders Safety Waders fame. May their creels be full. . . .

BUG DOPE

IDENTIFYING THOSE THINGS STUCK IN THE RADIATOR

By Staff Naturalist
Professor Millard Webbish

European Luftmothra

Greater Chameleon
(Fabula rasa)

Closet Gargyle

Irish Clippon

English Stonedhinge

Lesser Antilles

Dwarf Pygmy

True Death's Head

Autumn Gorgeous
(Lepidoptera Emaciata)

True Atlas

False Atlas

Common Brownie
(Adult Shutterbug)

Rosewindow
(Ambiguous religioso)

Upholsterer's Buttontuft

Yellow Delicious

Texas Behemoth

TIPS

When ya head out this deer season, try a couple a tricks the ol' timers swear by. First, pin a white rag or an ol' hankie down on the back o' yer lucky huntin' jacket. That's so's any deer a comin' up from behind will think yer one of 'em! It might jus' getcha that extry second ya need to put meat in the freezer! 'Nother thing ya can do is getcha an ol' set o' antlers an' wire 'em up so's ya can wear 'em like a hat! That's a sure-fire fooler for those big ol' woods-wise "rackers"! Use both o' these here tricks an' we guaran-damn-tee your luck'll change. . . .

—The Editors

NOTE: *HOOK & BULLET* has been running this gem just before deer season every year since 1900! Why someone would actually try this is beyond me; after all, there's no such thing as luck.

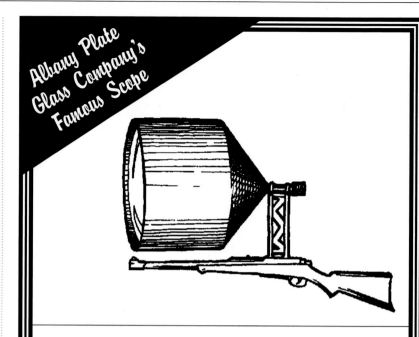

Albany Plate Glass Company's Famous Scope

THE PALOMAR PEEPER   1930

Note: The world's brightest scope measured a phenomenal 4 x 480 mm! While few disputed company claims that "when using a 'Palomar Peeper' you can see a buck earlier at dawn or later at dusk than with any other scope!" Fewer still could carry a "Peeper"-equipped rifle more than 20 yards at a time. The fact that one had to shoot from the hip while sighting through the scope did not help, either. Users were warned not to look at the sun.

HOW TO LAST A LIFETIME

ca. 1980

Percy Stence
(*Hook & Bullet* Survival Skills Editor)

◆ ◆ ◆

*H*ook & Bullet regrets to inform its readers that Mr. Stence will no longer be writing for us as he perished while on assignment researching his upcoming article, "Death Valley—Paradise or Hell? It's Up to You!"

*H*E WILL BE MISSED a little, but actually he wasn't all that much with a gun or a fly rod, either.

—The Editors

Two-Season Blinders

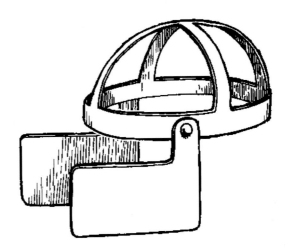

HUNTING

This is great for use while pheasant hunting with your brother-in-law, it allows you to forget about the direction of his shotgun and lets you concentrate on the dog.

FISHING

You can ignore that twelve-year-old 15 yards to your right who has landed his third 14-inch trout in half an hour using pink marshmallows on a dime-store rod! You are free to study the amber light caressing your split bamboo rod, which cost six times what you paid for your first car. The blinders weigh about as much as your empty reel.

from
Tunnelvision Products
Sleepy Eye, Minn.

ca. 1980

HOOK & BULLET

$.75
EGYPT $15

OCTOBER, 1967

DO BIGHORN SHEEP WATCH EWE OR YOU!

Peak Paranoia—The Other Altitude Sickness No One Talks About...

HOOK & BULLET

$1
TIBET $16.

MARCH 1969

BEARANOIA!

ARE *THEY* WATCHING YOU?
TIPS FROM A SHRINK THAT'LL HELP TAKE THE
TERROR OUT OF THE TIMBER (PAGE 91)

HOOK & BULLET

$1
TIBET $16.

1973

THE
BUCKAROO!!
IS THIS AUSTRALIAN/AMERICAN HYBRID THE ULTIMATE GAME?

HOOK & BULLET

$2.00

OHIO $14.61

APRIL 1977

CAMP COOKING NIGHTMARES!

How half cooked, greasy, overspiced meals full of ashes, dirt, and dead moths can affect your sleep!

Killer Whale Milk!

Claude Baulz

- **Aphrodisiac?**
- **Changes Human Odor into Natural Buck Lure?**
- **Fact or Fiction**
- **Is It Worth It? You Be the Judge!**

NOTE: *Hook & Bullet* regrets that Mr. Baulz has not been heard from since he wired in Part One of this story from Sitka, Alaska. We will publish Part Two, "The Milk Run" when we receive it. . . .

—The Editors
ca. June 1929

READY! AIM! FIRE! FIRE! FIRE! FIRE! FIRE! FIRE!

★ ★ ★ ★ ★ ★ ★ ★ ★ ★

With the All-New 1928

OSWEGO GUN WORKS 50-SHOT REVOLVER

The *HOLDZ-A-BOX* *.32 Special*

"YOU CAN SHOOT 'TIL YOUR FINGER HURTS"

CAUTION: FANNING THE HAMMER CAN RESULT IN CENTRIFUGAL FORCES SUFFICIENT TO MAKE AIMING IMPOSSIBLE.

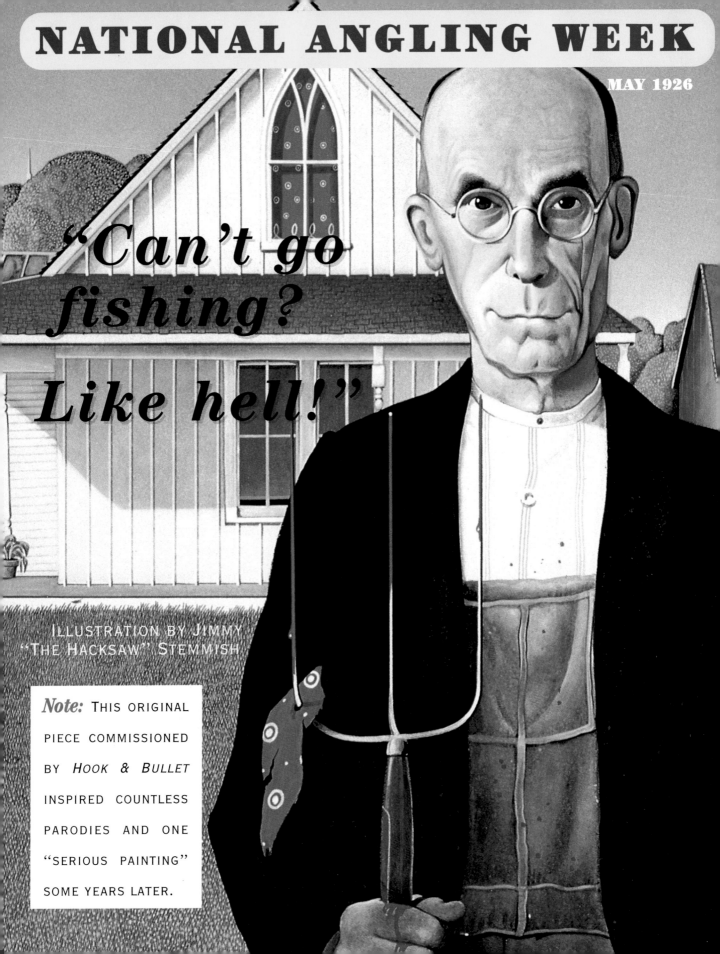

Grizzly Milk!

Claude Baulz

- **Aphrodisiac?**
- **Changes Human Odor into Natural Buck Lure?**
- **Fact or Fiction**
- **Is It Worth It? You Be the Judge!**

NOTE: Hook & Bullet wishes a speedy recovery for Mr. Baulz, a great editor and a fine hunting chum. "You're a braver man than I, Gungha Din!"

—The Editors
ca. June 1935

Mountain Lion Milk!

Claude Baulz

- **Aphrodisiac?**
- **Changes Human Odor into Natural Buck Lure?**
- **Fact or Fiction**
- **Is It Worth It? You Be the Judge!**

NOTE: Hook & Bullet lost a great editor and a fine hunting chum when Mr. Baulz disappeared while doing a follow-up article in Idaho.

—The Editors
ca. June 1936

TIRED OF DRAGGING DEER?

Do you constantly pass up monster bucks because, "Gosh! He's just too big to drag!"? Do taxidermists only charge you "rodent rates" because you can't drag in anything heavier than a ferret?

Change all that with a Hindenbuck—The World's Best Helium Bladder Deer Drag! Just slip the 125-lb. all-steel compressed-helium tank on your shoulder and you are ready to hunt. When that trophy buck is down, simply field dress him, insert the Hindenbuck's All-Rubber Lifting Bladder, and open the valve! In only seconds your deer will be bobbing along behind you on your way back to camp and your envious hunting pals! It's as easy as 1-2-3!

Tell your sporting good proprietor,
"I'll take a Hindenbuck every time!"

125 LB. HELIUM TANK

ALL-RUBBER BLADDER

For a **FREE** *90-page catalog, write:*

HINDENBUCK
c/o Deerigable Enterprises
Dept. BL-IMP
Lakehurst, New Jersey USA

ca. 1936

THE
RED OAKS
Est. 1902

Red Oaks

The Sportsman's Paradise

Guy Sousa

THE FABLED RED OAKS LODGE OF TANGIPA-HOA, Louisiana, has been awarded the coveted Alswythe-Jensen eight-star rating for the twenty-first consecutive year! When one considers that no other North American hunting lodge has ever garnered that prestigious rating more than four times and that Red Oaks is open to the public but one month per year, it is a truly astonishing feat.

Built in 1840 by Jean-François Chataignier, the New Orleans shipping magnate, the lodge was then known far and wide as Les Chênes Rouges, a 30,000-acre plantation gracing the banks of the beautiful Tangipahoa River. Sadly, it did not escape the ravages of the Civil War and was left severely damaged. After the war, Jean-François' ambitious plans to return the lodge to its former glory were only partially realized by the time of his death in 1874. While the main house and most of the ancillary buildings had been impeccably restored at the staggering cost of $6.5 million, the land had been largely ignored and the fields that were once so productive were reclaimed by Nature and became merely extensions of the dark woods that had surrounded them.

Guy Chataignier, Jean-François' only son, inherited both the family's steamship line and Les Chênes Rouges; however, he did not possess his father's talent for business and was forced to sell both five years later. The new owner, Staunton Hayes Davis, reveled in the business world, and fell in love with the idyllic grace of Les Chênes Rouges, which he renamed Red Oaks. There he could escape the pressures of his hectic life and, as he so often said, ". . . contemplate those truths which become apparent to one only in the presence of Nature."

In the year 1902, as a "present to the nation from a grateful American family," Staunton Hayes Davis opened Red Oaks to the public for the entire month of October. It was his desire that each ensuing October "the everyday sportsman would, for a time, be able to share in the best of the outdoors." Today, that tradition continues, thanks to the generosity of Staunton Hayes Davis IV and his family.

Guests pay a nominal fee of $1,700 per day to help cover basic operating costs of the facility. The fee has deterred few, as the lodge's twenty suites are currently booked through October of 2000. There is also a standby list containing the names of over 3,100 individuals hoping to be chosen at random should some unfortunate party cancel.

WHAT IS SO beguiling to sportsmen about Red Oaks that they would wait up to fifty years for a reservation? Is it the exquisite woodwork found in every suite, from glistening floors containing inlaid hunting scenes in exotic woods to the bounding game animals adorning each carved oak door? Is it the priceless collection of original sporting art that greets guests at every turn, or perhaps the Red Oaks library, its leather-bound volumes bathed in amber light from stained-glass windows?

Or could it be the ambiance of the Great Hall, where guests dine in splendor, as portraits of celebrated Red Oaks visitors, dressed in the hunting and fishing attire of the day, look on?

No. Important as these exceptional features are, they are but a part of the magic of Red Oaks, which is beloved not merely for its physical beauty and opulence but for its abundance of game. This is most apparent in the Red Oaks combination hunting and fishing quest known as "Tails and Scales." During October for thirty-three years, guests have roamed the wilds of their spectacular setting in search of the game duo synonymous with Red Oaks Lodge—world-class opossum and carp.

As a high point of this exciting and challenging event, participants are treated to the culinary artistry of Red Oaks Chef Master Michel la Verendrye. Each evening he delights the palate with a different entree celebrating the sumptuous possibilities of the renowned fish-and-game combination. Later, guests retire to the Gun Room for brandy and fellowship by the crackling fire. Truly, this is a sportsman's paradise!

NOTE: Regrettably, Red Oaks is now but a golden memory. On October 6, 1935, the magnificent lodge and surrounding trees were leveled by the massive explosion of the carp and opossum steamer used by Master Chef la Verendrye to prepare his famous Red Oaks Crème Sauce. All that remained of the outdoorsmen's Eden was a blackened crater and a scattering of tails and scales.
Paradise was lost.

—The Editors

TWICE THE STOCK!
HALF THE RECOIL!

THE NORTLE BI-STOCK

YOU'VE GOT TWO SHOULDERS
USE 'EM !!

AUGUST						
		1	2	3	4	5
6	7	8	9	10	11	12
13	14	15	16	17	18	19
20	21	22	23	24	25	26
27	28	29	30	31	See catalog for Information	

19   35

Your First Dog!

Backyard Breeders and Discount Dogs

GARTH CALFRIPPER

- How to Choose
- Do's & Don'ts
- Sure He's Cute, But Will He Hunt?
- Hot Tips from Guys in the Know

NOTE: Over the years *Hook & Bullet* received thousands of requests for reprints of this helpful article. By popular demand it was published again in May 1972 under the title, "Get Away from Me!" It appeared again in 1981 as "They Don't All Eat the Decoys (Or, How to Buy a Better Dog!)" and yet again in 1991 as "Backyard Breeders = Canine Criminals?"　　　ca. April 1957

"Thar Whatever-It-Is Blows!"

Hook & Bullet Does Its Part in the Cold War!

ISHMAEL RICKOVER

July 1959

The Pentagon has requested that *Hook & Bullet* alert its readers (particularly those in the Northwest) to this insidious national-security threat. It seems that salmon and halibut fishermen operating in the waters between Seattle and the Queen Charlotte Islands have begun reporting an unusually large killer whale. WARNING: It is not an oversize orca but a Soviet spy submarine known as SHAMU (Submarine Hull Alternative for Maneuvering Unnoticed). Pentagon spokesmen are saying little about the craft beyond the fact that it is "a mechano-nuclear reconnaissance submersible served by a highly trained 37-man crew," and civilians are cautioned strongly that, "If SHAMU is observed or found washed up on a beach, CALL AUTHORITIES IMMEDIATELY!"

YOU BETCHA!

—The Editors

POSTSCRIPT:

Shortly after that issue of *Hook & Bullet* hit the newsstands, a then-unknown sister spy ship was discovered to have been "captured" in the Strait of Juan de Fuca by the Squidland Aquatic Park vessel *Pequod*! The SHAMU had already been performing three shows daily before a retired navy chief petty officer spotted rust on the whale's hull and became suspicious.

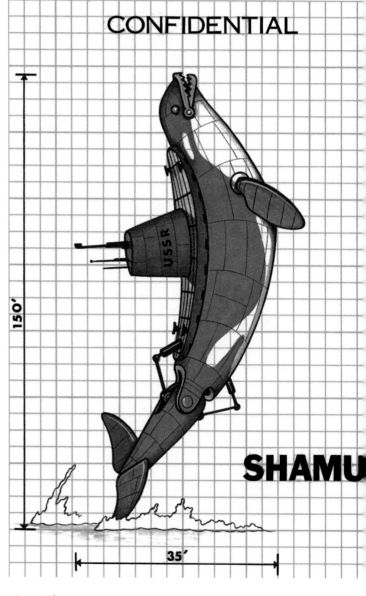

CONFIDENTIAL

150'

USSR

35'

SHAMU

Everglades Moose!

The Ultimate Challenge?

SOUTHERN EDITOR MARSUPIAL J. CLAXTON

Tells You How, When, and Where!

Much controversy arose over this story (Aug. 1956)—or, we should say, over the painting commissioned to accompany it. While some suggested that the subject was old hat, more were upset about the depiction of a canoeist not wearing a life vest! Subsequent stories (twenty-six of them) about hunting Everglades moose were always illustrated with the hunter wearing a life vest—blaze orange of course.

HELL'S ANGLERS

From the fiery bowels of the earth, a new breed of fly fishermen has emerged . . . and they mean business.

By Henry Rose Stifwyck

Fly fishermen will sure be in for a shock when they see who else has taken up their quiet, contemplative pastime. I'm afraid our blue-ribbon trout streams are no longer a safe haven for tweedy, Latin-babbling elitists and wadered wimps fretting whether a strike indicator is a bobbler or not. No, my fastidious friends, you pusillanimous purists are about to get a dose of reality right in the middle of your aesthetic experience. You thought you were serious fishermen? Wait till you meet . . . Hell's Anglers!

That's right—Hell's Anglers: fly-fishing, hog-straddling, septic-breathed bikers who would think nothing of tearing off your pre-washed adventurer jacket and using it to wipe down their "rides." Led by Eddie "Rat Face" McDougal, these rapacious renegades of the riffles travel streamside roads 300 strong, winding through the landscape single-file like a thundering, voracious, chrome-plated, trout-devouring serpent. When they see a rise they stop, check their teeth, and then match the hatch. The results are devastating! In just minutes entire river sections are gang-fished out. They move on in a blue carbon monoxide haze, leaving in their fetid wake only sterile, oil-slicked waters and once-tranquil hillsides reverberating with the echoes of unbridled American iron.

No, pal, you won't find those trendy teal or magenta fly vests in this hook-heaving horde from Hades. Their fishing fashion statement is made with black bullhide, zippers, studs, and a couple of rows of bullet loops. Their licenses have walnut grips, they get their fleece patches off live sheep, cut their tippets and trim their knots with a 7-inch Randall fighting knife, and they know their outfit is balanced when the weight of the fly line matches their I.Q. Sure, they may think Izaak Walton was one of John-Boy's uncles, but beware, you laugh at them once and they'll convert your Audi with its "I ♥ Montana" bumper sticker into a diving bell.

Yessir, all those years of manhan-

ca. 1960

HELL'S ANGLERS

dling half a ton of two-wheeled screaming steel has given them arms that can put blood knots in a tire iron and roll cast an anvil. We're talking primordial flesh-eaters, double-hauling locusts who see "catch and release" as a cheap excuse to spare pantywaists from cleaning fish, so don't worry yourself about any silly stream etiquette. Even if you have a fish on, just hand over your rod and leave. Avoid eye contact and don't even think about asking, "Mind if I fish through?"—you'll end up inside your own rod tube. I'm telling you, friend, they'll take your head off so fast you'll think there was a ferrule in your neck.

Look what happened when Hell's Anglers found Alton Hastings III fishing a spring creek in western Montana. He was never the same. Now white-haired with hollow eyes perpetually locked in a thousand-yard stare, the thirty-one-year-old former dry-fly snob spends his days sitting in front of a Livingston fly shop reading bass magazines and eating Chinese take-out. His bamboo chopsticks with the silk-wrapped snake guides are all that remain of the custom rod he had flaunted from the Battenkill to the Big Hole.

There's no telling where or when Hell's Anglers will strike. One day you'll be fishing and think you heard distant thunder, but when the rumble swells and builds into a throbbing, rock-splitting cacophony of detonations, there will be no doubt—it's them! When they stop they won't ask, "Have any luck?" They already know . . . it just ran out.

My advice to you fly-fishing readers is this: Stay away from any decent trout stream! Think of your loved ones—it's just not worth it! Start playing handball again, or take up golf. Let me check out places like the Madison, Gallatin, Yellowstone, and the Green. I'll let you know when it's safe. . . .

DAFFY DUCK HUNTING

Now, for the first time in print, the gear waterfowlers really used in the good old days . . .

By Trenfell G. Fezmer

No one I've ever met knew as much about the outdoors as Wollard Grandpap Wheet. He devoted his life to hunting and fishing, and I was privileged to spend many of my early years learning at his side. Some of Grandpap's friends called his duck-hunting tactics a bit unorthodox—some even called them daffy—but that never deterred him. And now, as another season begins, I think back on those many days I shared with him on the flyway—and realize I should share Grandpap's favorite gear with the readers of this fine magazine. He would have wanted it that way. Thanks, Grandpap Wheet. . . .

The MM-66 Mallard Mortar, ca. 1933

This creation of the B. L. Sparvey Flare and Fireworks Factory located in Wilmington, Delaware, was eventually used by virtually every waterfowler in the country, until changes in federal legislation made it all but impossible to get the required Class III Sport Mortar license. Though simple, the Mallard Mortar was incredibly effective. Basically, there were two parts: 1) the ordi-

nance steel mortar tube, and 2) the decoy rocket. The latter was nothing more than a cluster of percussion-fired blackpowder propellants with a duck-head assembly at one end, an exhaust nozzle at the other, and a pair of spring-loaded wings in the middle. The entire assembly was covered in a duck paint scheme, one

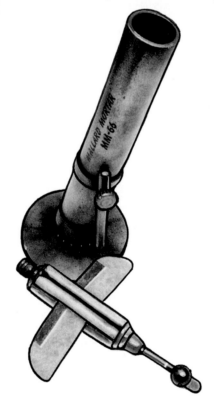

of six species available. Fired in the usual mortar fashion, the Mallard Mortar sent a decoy rocket hurtling skyward in an arching trajectory through high-flying flocks of wary ducks. At that point, it would appear to the ducks to be one of their number peeling off to land on the water below. That image was further enhanced by a dual-reed call in the projectile's head, which produced a loud, prolonged quaaaaaaaaaaaaccck that lasted for the duration of the flight. A majority of the flock always followed, and a skillful hunter with a properly adjusted tube could bring them to within 15 feet of a blind. After splashdown, the spent rocket was retrieved by the hunter's canine companion, to be recharged with powder and sent aloft again and again as needed.

In those days it was not uncommon for wealthier sportsmen to own several mortars, spending the weeks before opening day busily loading decoys. Thus armed with dozens of decoy rockets, they could send up a volley, easily convincing ducks that half the flock was doing a slow roll and going in. The only drawback to the Mallard Mortar invariably occurred when someone in another

Grandpap Wheet would have wanted his favorite gear shared with the readers of Hook & Bullet.

blind and unfamiliar with the invention opened fire as the "duck" headed skyward. The resulting secondary explosions from such a hit blew the decoys to smithereens and sent more than one confused hunter home early to sit out the rest of the season in his den. A few even swore off bourbon and sold their dogs.

Dunphey Brothers Model 14 Dual-Valve Pintail Bugle, ca. 1920

The largest and by far the loudest call ever to enter production, the Bugle was most popular in the Northeast, where hunting pressure was great even in the halcyon days of the 1920s. The dual valves afforded easy mastery of a feed call, but more important was the sound level. Ads for the Model 14 suggested that "Now you can hunt in the most crowded section of the flyway, and the birds will only notice you! Get their attention while they're still over the horizon with a roaring 1.5 Db feed call!" The Db referred to Duckibel, or unit of sound required to

startle a sleeping wigeon three miles away. By contrast, most calls of that era were .25 Db.

While initial purchasers enjoyed a distinct advantage over fellow waterfowlers, it was short-lived, as production quickly caught up with demand and virtually every blind east of the Mississippi was armed with a Pintail Bugle. Unfortunately, the combined din from 30 to 40 blinds in proximity was so intense that few souls could tolerate more than an hour of hunting.

Labraduck Kamo Kit, 1911

Is there any duck hunter who doesn't go afield without strapping his dog into one of these? You're right, of course not; but back in 1911 the only thing a dog carried to the blind was fleas. That is until R. "Big Bob" Nolte of Savannaville, Illinois, made a startling observation. Nolte had just finished another luckless day of hunting and was packing up all of his camouflage gear when he realized that his dog was the reason why ducks were flaring off at the last second. Of course! "Big Bob" had discovered the secret to successful duck hunting: Make your dog blend in too! He soon perfected and began marketing the now-famous Labraduck Kamo Kit. With this, a full-grown retriever could go undetected by waterfowl, be unhampered by the hinged beak, and actually be given added buoyancy thanks to the

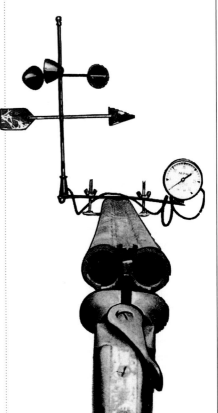

plywood wings. Today the Noltes continue to produce Labraduck Kamo Kits with the same attention to detail they are so famous for. The line has been expanded, with different sizes added to include German Shepherd retrievers and poodle retrievers. The beaks are standard yellow/orange, but today's hunter may order wings in teal, mallard, redhead, goldeneye, and coot.

Breez-O-Meter, ca. 1928

This ingenious device was designed to take the guesswork out of lateral deflection by measuring even the slightest gust right at the point where windage begins—the muzzle. Once the device was clamped to the barrel(s), a quick glance from the front sight bead told the shooter wind direction and wind speed, thus enabling him to compensate at the

very last microsecond. The Breez-O-Meter was constructed entirely of marine brass and weighed three pounds, which further aided the shooter by reducing muzzle jump and felt recoil.*

The same company produces the Breez-O-Meter today, with few changes from the highly successful original. They are still made of marine brass to withstand the cold, wet weather so typical of duck season; however, a modern LED MPH/Clock/Calculator has replaced the old familiar dial. The company slogan is as appropriate in 1986 as it was nearly sixty years ago: "Check The Breeze Before You Squeeze!"

Merrimac Steam-Powered Shot-Proof Decoy, ca. 1860

This example of the iron-decoy maker's craft was produced shortly after the Civil War and represents a type of decoy seldom seen in use today. Once extremely popular, they were designed for the novice sportsman whose constant low shots played havoc with carved wooden decoys. Direct hits to a Merrimac merely chipped at the paint, while the sloped iron side deflected the lead shot harmlessly skyward.

Though costing 14 times as much as a wooden decoy, the steam decoy not only lasted years longer but also possessed the additional feature of motion. Once the gear was placed in F (Forward) and the throttle and rudder adjusted, a Merrimac could chuff about in front of a blind for just under an hour—easily convincing any duck overhead to join him. In this decoy's heyday, it was not uncommon for a hunter to be shooting over a set of 30 to 40 Merrimacs busily paddling about in circles in front of the blind.

Though there are reports of decoy boilers blowing and subsequent fires destroying blinds, it was not that danger which finally caused

them to lose favor with sportsmen. In 1904 scientists linked the Merrimacs' hull primer paint (Pb304) to lead poisoning in waterfowl. Thus ended what must be regarded as the most enchanting era in the history of decoy manufacturing.

(For more information about steam-powered shot-proof decoys, contact either the William F. Merrimac Steam Decoy Museum or Rivet World; both are located in Pittsburgh, Pennsylvania.)

The Skylab Company Dog Launcher, ca. 1922

"You down your duck but your dog won't budge because it's 26°F, wind out of the west at 37 mph, and the water is so cold there's skim ice? Next time put some spring in your pooch with a Skylab Dog Launcher—the reluctant retriever remedy!"

Thus read the advertising copy for one of the most effective pieces of gear to come out of the 1920s. It

was a marvel of simplicity, yet eminently effective. The launcher was screwed into the ground by means of the pigtail rod affixed to its base, then the two steel pivot clamps were ratcheted down onto the launch seat through the use of the ratchet/release lever until they compressed the powerful launch spring. The retriever was then placed directly upon the seat and centered on the black X. This final step was necessary because the dog would have a tendency to hook or slice should it be off center. Once a duck was dropped, the hunter issued the retrieve command; then, if the dog failed to respond, the ratchet/release lever was twisted clockwise and thrust forward, thereby freeing the two pivot clamps and subsequently altering the stubborn canine's point of view. A wiser retriever would soon return with duck in mouth.

Because the Skylab Dog Launcher came in four sizes, hunters were cautioned to buy the correct size for their particular retriever. Obviously a small dog on a launcher designed for Labs could create a problem.

Due to the unusually warm fall seasons of 1924 and 1925, dogs balked less, demands for the launchers plummeted, and in 1926 the overextended Skylab Dog Launcher Company went bankrupt.

Then, in 1942, President Roosevelt appealed to all patriotic American hunters to aid the war effort by turning over any Skylab Dog Launchers they still had. These were eventually used by the navy for ejection-seat research, development, and training.

*Felt Recoil—the degree of shoulder pain experienced through a one-half-inch felt pad after 10 rounds.

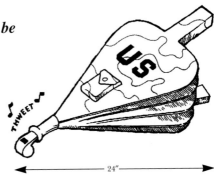

THE IMPROVED WHITETAIL

Deer hunting can be a tough, humbling experience. What if bucks could be altered to make it easier for us?

By Clemmish Rebbil, Jr.

Over the years I've sat around a lot of campfires listening to exasperated hunters' dissertations on deer. Haggard and luckless at the end of a long day, they lament about different bucks they heard but couldn't see; bucks that exploded from the brush at their elbow, leaving them alone in a vast silence, dazed and shaking, with their rifles no closer to their shoulders than before. Wistfully, they've gone on about those bucks that got away; ten-pointers fast enough to qualify for pole position at the Indy 500; big, wary old bucks that could hear a rifle rusting in a rainstorm and spook at least 2 miles away if a hunter's eyes even dilate.

INDEED, deer hunting can be a tough, humbling experience. Is there some way we could change that? Equipment can't get much better, but what about the deer?

FOR STARTERS, everyone wants a nice buck, so what if the average whitetail were a twenty-pointer (typical), weighing in at 1,700 pounds dressed, and had hooves like a Clydesdale? That would help slow the bucks down a bit, and tracking them would sure be easier! At that size, their stealth quotient would be about the same as a rhino dragging Venetian blinds through a rock quarry.

ALSO, DEER don't come in the easiest color to spot. Chartreuse would be much better, and it would simplify things in the woods—hunters are bright orange; deer, bright green.

WHAT ABOUT A deer's spectacular eyesight and incredible hearing? It might be better if their ears were smaller and their eyes were about as good as a fruit bat's. Maybe their nose should be so ineffective that they couldn't detect a swimming pool full of ammonia at 10 feet.

THINK about it!

THE IMPROVED WHITETAIL
(continued)

AFTER ALL THOSE changes, whitetails would certainly be a lot different . . . but then so would hunting.

TRUE, YOU might get a rack that you could do chin-ups from and tenderloin steaks the size of hubcaps, but where's the challenge, the thrill, the pride of accomplishment, or the exhilaration of the hunt? Where could you get a carpet for your trophy room that didn't clash?

WHEN I REALLY think about it, I like deer just the way they are—unimproved.

-TIP-

Many of today's hunters realize that having a radio in your treestand can really help pass those long boring hours and postpone all those negative "what the hell am I doing here" thoughts. However, it's real important to keep the volume down—your batteries will last a lot longer!

ca. 1983

THE NIMROD GAMES

Baseball has the World Series, football has the Super Bowl, but hunters and fishermen have their own premier tournament!

By Irving Sneff

In the realm of sport there are a few competitions whose hallowed names represent the pinnacle of human endeavor to all who hear them: the World Series, the Super Bowl, and the Biloxi Float-Offs for Synchronized Swimming.

ABOVE THEM ALL, however, is the premier tournament for the serious sportsman—the Nimrod Games. Begun during the mountain-man rendezvous of the early 1800s, this is a quadrennial gathering of the world's finest hunters and fishermen competing in fifty events. For example, there is the Plano Put where angler-athletes must scream, "I lost him!" before hurling a fully loaded 35-pound tackle box into a racing pool for distance.

THERE IS ALSO the Duck Huntathalon. In this event, shivering contestants in plaid wool jumpsuits each hold a thrashing Labrador retriever overhead while bobbing about in ice water up to their chins, their violet lips blowing on duck calls hard enough to shred the reeds. It's a thrilling elimination contest, for the winner is the last man treading water whose dog is warm and dry!

AS A SEASONED deer hunter, a favorite of mine is a demanding two-part contest—the Biathalong Haul. Before dawn the hunter-athlete must consume a large plate of greasy food, drink two thermoses of thick black coffee, run in place for ten minutes, assemble a treestand, and ascend with it up a telephone pole to a mark 50 feet above the ground. There he must remain motionless for exactly six hours before shooting off-hand, with a sandwich clenched between his teeth, at a bottle of Hot Doe Scent placed 100 yards downrange. In part two of the competition, the athlete must freefall to the ground, then affix a short piece of nylon rope to a 200-pound slab of cement and drag it a half mile through a sand pit. The winner is the man who doesn't lose his car keys.

MY ALL-TIME favorite event is the 440 X 16 Adams, otherwise known as "The Sprint to the Stream." In a reverse Le Mans start, six competitors are packed in a station wagon at the starting line. When the official screams, "We're here!", the racers leap from the vehicle, dash to the rear of the car, sort out and don clothing, and then assemble a three-piece fly rod. Thus attired in full fishing regalia, the galloping anglers race

furiously around the ¼-mile track leaping over hurdles while suffusing the stadium with the thrum and screech of sweat-soaked neoprene. They arrive at fly-tying benches with their legs chafed, their arms jellied, and temples throbbing hard enough to bend the frames of their fogged-up polarized glasses. Next, they race to tie a No. 16 Adams and affix it to their 8X tippet. The event is won by the angler whose single cast is thrown the closest to a target 50 feet away—an open 6-ounce jar of pork rinds. This race is much more than a grueling athletic endeavor—it is a metaphor echoing the experience of everyone who has ever fished with friends.

FROM THE LIGHTING of the Coleman Lamp at the opening ceremony to the poignant closing when the lamp is kicked over and the mantle broken, the Nimrod Games are the epitome of outdoor sport. And best of all, virtually all outdoorsmen are perpetually in training for these Games—whether they realize it or not.

EPHEMERA RAPTORUS

By Cardiff L. Smott

The nightmare began in the spring of 1930 on the Idaho-Montana border, in a secret cabin owned by famed entomologist and avid fly fisherman, Dr. Harold H. Green, former head of the Insect Observation Division at M.I.T. (Missoula Insect Trap Co., the largest manufacturer of flypaper, envelope glue, and artificially flavored pancake syrup in the world). For two decades, until his firing for suspected theft of company equipment, Dr. Green's responsibility at M.I.T. had been to sit on the R&D porch documenting thousands of gnats, midges, and blowflies doing deep knee bends in the glutinous surface of experimental fly strips dangling over tubs of aging ground round.

As one might well imagine, the physical and emotional strain of such a demanding job took a toll on Dr. Green's psyche. However, it was his humiliating dismissal from the company that left him a disturbed man. Bitter, moody, and withdrawn, he no longer found solace in his beloved fly fishing, for his once-steady hands now shook so violently that he couldn't thread a 7X tippet through the hole of a doughnut. His elegant casting style had deteriorated to the point where his presentation of a minuscule size 28 dry

disturbed more water than a lobbed cinder block. Even spotting the take of a sipping trout at 30 yards with his overstrained eyes was out of the question—at that distance, he couldn't make out a Great White hammering a seal.

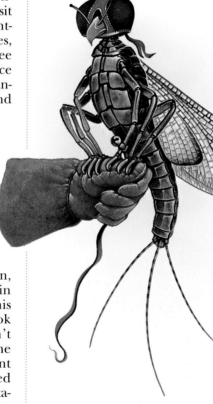

Nevertheless, the stress-crazed genius was not about to abandon fly fishing. Instead he would employ the remaining sparks of his twisted brilliance to conceive a bizarre new technique for taking trout.

"I am convinced," Dr. Green wrote in his journal, "that all mayflies possess genetic knowledge of being trout food for the past 500,000 years—and, no doubt, they resent it. I shall capitalize on that fact by breeding them to a size that will enable me to benefit from their inherited grudge."

Using the millions of dollars worth of laboratory equipment he had filched from M.I.T., Green set about exploiting the humble mayfly for his shameful purpose. But who knows how he achieved the hyper-accelerated mayfly reproductive cycles? Who among us can imagine what vile concoction, putrid potion, or wretched ray was used to distort the growth genes of the initial mayfly eggs percolating in his evil incubators?

Whatever technique Green used, it worked, for on June 18 he wrote, "This morning I transferred my first batch of 'treated' eggs to the nearby spring creek and watched them transform into nymphs the size of crayfish. This afternoon a dozen glorious

2-pound mayflies suddenly burst through the water's surface like a flushed covey of olive drab quail!"

BY EARLY JULY, Dr. Green's modified mayflies were much bigger. "I am on the right track! The flies are laying eggs the size of guavas! In a matter of hours the streambed crawls with nymphs that look like Maine lobsters, and then become even larger flying creatures than their parents! To match this hatch," Green wrote, "I'd need a feather duster wired to a meat hook."

THE UNSETTLING entry of July 12 at last makes the sinister purpose of Dr. Green abundantly clear: "I spent the afternoon watching my fabulous flies take their revenge. Dozens of them hovered and plummeted into the water, snatching up and devouring rainbows like a flock of starving, six-legged osprey. Indeed, these flies do catch trout! I have named them Ephemerella Raptorus, and now I can train them like birds of prey during the Middle Ages. They shall do my fishing for me! I call this new sport . . . flyconry."

DR. GREEN'S demented joy proved premature, for he soon learned a hard lesson: tampering with Nature is as dangerous as driving a golf ball in a tile bathroom—there are just too many angles to figure. On the thirteenth week his experiment literally flew out of control. He was suddenly powerless to stop the process he had begun! From the safety of his cabin/laboratory, Dr. Green watched, confused and horrified, as freak flies grown twice the size of a turkey buzzard worked thermals high in the clear skies before folding their wings and plunging

into the water to nail panicked salmonids at 200 mph. Hundreds of others stalked, strutted, and gorged at the edge of his soon-to-be-sterile spring creek.

THAT SAME DAY, eight miles away, the terrorized residents of Scruttville, Montana (pop. 1,143), huddled in their homes, prisoners of 4,000 mammoth mayflies that perched on roofs, fences, cars, trees, and telegraph wires. Their multifaceted eyes sought out anything edible—fish, stray cats, dogs, cattle, and, yes—people.

THEN, JUST AS swiftly as it began . . . it ended. The immense insects literally disappeared overnight. Did they migrate elsewhere to avoid a Montana winter? Did they all die attempting to cross the Rockies and get into some decent steelhead? One can only guess. . . .[1]

SCRUTTVILLE DIED. The residents fled, never to return, and little if any evidence of that sad town remains today. The trauma still haunts the folks up on that Idaho border, but they refuse to discuss it. "Scruttville? Never heard of it!" they'll tell you, all the while casting a wary eye skyward just to make sure any gliding form in the distance is only a hawk.[2]

WHAT BECAME OF the infamous Dr. Harold H. Green? He was run out of the state by vigilantes after they covered him with tar and feathers, which ironically gave him the appearance of an oversized dun. The winds of time finally blew out his pilot light in 1947 at his home in Death Valley, a fly-strip–festooned trailer where he finished his paranoid years under the name Orlando A. Hitchcock. He was as far from water as he could get.

[1]Today, Montana's largest mayflies, though no longer the size of ducks, are still referred to as "Green Drakes."

[2]In the early '60s a movie based on the Scruttville siege became a horror classic. The type of winged creatures depicted in the story were changed, however. Hence the movie title, "The Bats."

ULTIMATE SURVIVAL GEAR

Would you even consider going into the backcountry without a Portable Hydro-Dam? Neither would any true woodsman.

By Ajax Packard

When is enough gear enough? "When what you take into the woods weighs as much as everything else left in your house," advises the grandson of legendary outdoorsman Wollard "Grandpap" Wheet. Here he shows us items he *always* takes with him, practical "must-have" gear for serious outdoorsmen.

TORFLETT BROTHERS HAND-POWERED CHAINSAW:

Why anyone would hit the trail without a Torflett Brothers Hand-Powered Chainsaw lashed to his pack is beyond me. There's no gas or oil to worry about, no fouled plugs, and none of that eardrum-searing din. Simply turn the crank and watch the chips fly. What could be easier? You say you arrived at Lake Squamitz after dark but still want to sit around a roaring

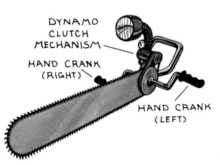

DYNAMO CLUTCH MECHANISM

HAND CRANK (RIGHT)

HAND CRANK (LEFT)

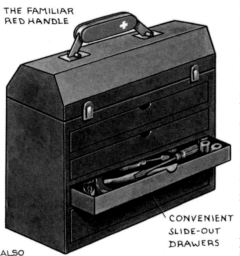

THE FAMILIAR RED HANDLE

CONVENIENT SLIDE-OUT DRAWERS

ALSO AVAILABLE IN WOODLAND GREEN OR CAMO

SAK 127
[127 TOOLS
[TOTAL WT. — 73 lbs.
[SAK 127 BELT POUCH (LEATHER)
[TOTAL WT. — 12 lbs.

campfire? No problem, pardner—merely engage the miniature dynamo-clutch mechanism, and on comes the handy worklight! The faster you saw, the more you see! It even comes with a snap-on red lens to help preserve your night vision. Folks, this item is a must for any survival kit.

SWISS ARMY KNIFE-127:

From my years in the brush, I know that once in a while even the best equipment breaks. It can be anything from a cross-threaded cap on a survival

knife to a broken firing pin in your semiautomatic flare gun. Don't let something like that spoil your expedition. Travel prepared with the one piece of equipment that can get you out of any jam: a Swiss Army Knife. We're not talking about the ones carried by Swiss privates here, either. What you need is the SAK-127, the one the lieutenants get. One word of caution: when carrying the knife in its belt pouch, wear suspenders.

KANTEENOLEER:

Have you ever been backpacking in the high desert and suddenly found yourself out of water, forced to eat your freeze-dried lunch right out of the envelope? Ever sat in the middle of nowhere staring at an empty canteen, munching on

EACH OF THE DOZEN CANTEENS IS EASILY REMOVED FOR REFILLING

CANTEEN COVERS ARE TOUGH O D NYLON

instant-coffee crystals, and wondering how you'll survive without water? Well, it's happened to me ... but not anymore!

Nowadays I take along Kanteenoleer, a new product that guarantees, "You'll Never Go Thirsty Again!" Each one carries a dozen U.S. Army-issue canteens—three gallons of water at your fingertips! That's enough to wash your socks and mix some powdered minestrone!

STEEL ARMADILLO BODY SHELL:

Like to camp but afraid of snakes? Like to fish but allergic to blackflies? Do you enjoy hiking but get annoyed by rain, wind, chiggers, and mosquitoes? Are you afraid to get into a stream because you've heard of leeches so big they can draw blood through waders? Relax! You don't have to live like that. Instead, slip into the new Steel Armadillo Body Shell. It really works! Just look at all the wonderful features designed to separate you from all the vipers and boonie bugs lurking out there. As you can see, absolutely nothing can penetrate this wilderness garment; in fact, it's even guaranteed to be wolverine-proof and lightning-resistant!

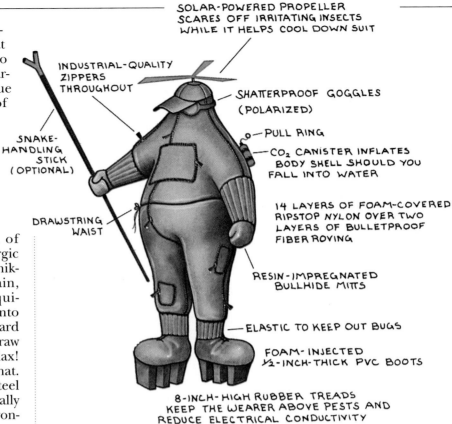

SOLAR-POWERED PROPELLER SCARES OFF IRRITATING INSECTS WHILE IT HELPS COOL DOWN SUIT

INDUSTRIAL-QUALITY ZIPPERS THROUGHOUT

SNAKE-HANDLING STICK (OPTIONAL)

DRAWSTRING WAIST

SHATTERPROOF GOGGLES (POLARIZED)

PULL RING

CO_2 CANISTER INFLATES BODY SHELL SHOULD YOU FALL INTO WATER

14 LAYERS OF FOAM-COVERED RIPSTOP NYLON OVER TWO LAYERS OF BULLETPROOF FIBER ROVING

RESIN-IMPREGNATED BULLHIDE MITTS

ELASTIC TO KEEP OUT BUGS

FOAM-INJECTED ½-INCH-THICK PVC BOOTS

8-INCH-HIGH RUBBER TREADS KEEP THE WEARER ABOVE PESTS AND REDUCE ELECTRICAL CONDUCTIVITY

PORTABLE HYDRO-DAM:

What about evenings in camp? You've hiked miles into the backcountry, set up your tent, and now the sun's gone down. There's nothing to see and nothing to listen to except crickets. Not much fun, huh? Why not take a television? Enjoying nature doesn't mean you have to miss *Wide World of Carp*. Feel like dancing? Take a tape deck! Now you can take anything you like—from halogen floodlights to your favorite electric wok. Sounds great, but am I talking about 370 pounds of batteries? No! I take a surplus Corps of Engineers portable hydroelectric dam. This fiberglass goody weighs a mere 30 pounds and comes in a neat OD storage bag. Wedge it into any ditch, and in minutes 110 volts are at your command! If you're lost, power a CB, then use the upstream side for recreation—boating, fishing, swimming—until help comes.

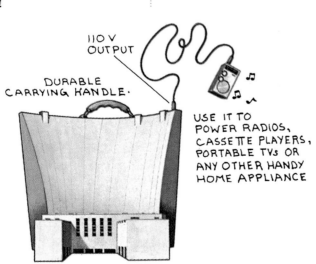

110 V OUTPUT

DURABLE CARRYING HANDLE.

USE IT TO POWER RADIOS, CASSETTE PLAYERS, PORTABLE TVs OR ANY OTHER HANDY HOME APPLIANCE

Reel of the Future

The System Telecast's capabilities are so spectacular, you'll want to mortgage your house to own one!

By Cranmore Hallup

A reel for the 21st century has arrived at last with the introduction of the revolutionary new System Telecast. Incorporating today's most sophisticated technology, this reel is so advanced that it makes all other reel designs obsolete. It is a milestone reminiscent of the bass boat breakthrough years ago when, overnight, fishing craft changed from flat-bottomed, plywood, green-hulled scows to high-speed, high-tech, metalflake fiberglass wonder boats—from state of the ark to state of the art!

So it is now with the System Telecast, the spectacular result of a $70-million, nine-year collaboration by engineering teams from three corporations whose CEO's belong to the same bass club. Southern Trotline (Atlanta-based manufacturer of telephone equipment), Nemodyne (research submarines), and Bassio (America's largest maker of diving watches) have brilliantly combined their expertise in fiber optics, monofilament technology, and ultramicro circuity to place critical fishing information right at the angler's thumb tip. A micro cam in the nose of the motorized lure sends images back to the reel's color television monitor. By manipulating the rudder, diving, and speed controls, the fisherman is able to search for his quarry and then steer his plug enticingly back and forth in front of the chosen bass, all the while following the action on closed-circuit television! The plug's underwater mike is coupled to a pair of stereo mini speakers in the reel's frame, allowing the angler to plainly hear everything going on down there.

The excitement can be preserved on the ultramicro cassette deck to be viewed again with friends. If that's not enough, information such as time, water temperature, and pH are conveniently displayed next to the screen, while wind direction, barometric pressure, and moon phase appear on the handle side. Want more? You get it, with a forty-channel CB added as a safety feature! What makes all this go, you ask? Power is supplied by a battery that gets recharged by a mini generator every time you crank in the lure! Folks, if it seems like the System Telecast does everything but clean your fish, you are almost right. But, what if there aren't any fish? No problem! Simply rotate the SELECT switch just below the drag, and your graphite rod is now functioning as a VHF antenna for standard television reception!

Yep—even if there are more fish in the Mojave than you've got near your boat on Great Carp Lake, you can sit on the water, rod in one hand, swatting mosquitoes with the other, and still watch Hank, Roland, and Orlando reelin' 'em in!

Yes, sir, I predict the System Telecast will be in every serious angler's tackle box, despite its $7,100 price tag!

Swap!

ART COLLECTOR POSSESSING 14 MAJOR EXAMPLES OF ABSTRACT EXPRESSIONISM SEEKS TRADE FOR SOMETHING USEFUL OR INTERESTING. DO YOU HAVE ANY PAINTINGS OF DOGS PLAYING POKER, DRINKING, CARVING DECOYS, OR TYING FLIES? HOW ABOUT AN ICE AUGER OR TROLLING MOTOR? LET'S TALK! H&B J71-T

ca. 1990

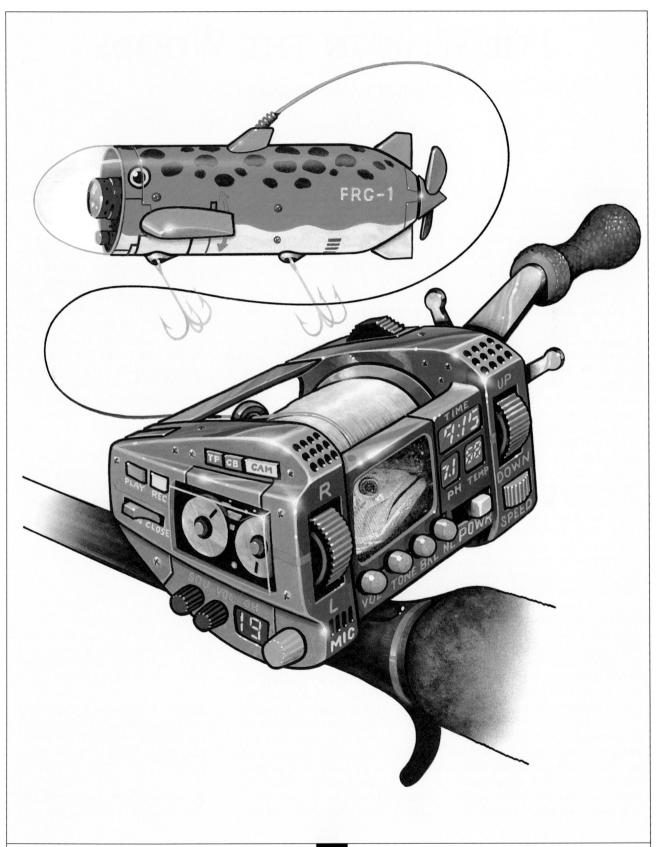

THE WIMP IN THE WOODS

By Clayton Shrapnel

Thrunson Bivalve Jones staggered down the trail under his immense load, his straining back bent so low that he received a constant barrage of stunning uppercuts from his own knees. Every tendon in his aching body felt as if it would soon tear free, like tripped-over lamp cords jerked from a socket. Sweat, mixed with black dye from the printed "zebra skin" band of his "affordable" safari hat, coursed down his face in dark parallel lines and filled the lenses of his replica WWI motorcycle goggles. The inky fluid sloshed slowly to and fro, transforming the eyewear into a bubble level for his head. Beneath his sodden adventurer jacket, its bullet loops full of "tactical" map markers, he wore a set of "NATO-style" camouflage fatigues, the splotchy apparel that gave him the appearance of being swaddled in a drop cloth from a tractor factory. His ultra-light "jungle style" boots had each become a thirty-pound bolus of mud and forest debris which he was unable to lift, forcing him to shuffle along, plowing the twin furrows that marked his trail. He would have surely fallen had it not been for the constant death grip he maintained on his "ninja black" anodized aluminum combination adventurers' walking stick and marshmallow skewer. At least poor Thrunson's torture would be over soon, for he was nearly at his campsite, a full 120 yards into the woods—farther in than he'd ever been before!

WAS THRUNSON scared? Not on your life, pal, for the massive burden compressing his vertebrae and reducing his feet to a pair of pink, five-toed flat irons was the very thing giving him confidence! Thrunson was sure he was safe, you see, because the 11,000-cubic-inch "elite forces night ops" HERNIA IV backpack contained nothing but survival gear! Yessir, Thrunson trundled through the timber with over 170 lbs. of "must have," "mill spec," "adventurer proven," "commando style," "special ops," "guaranteed to last a lifetime" equipment, and he'd ordered it all from the wimps' dream book—the SURPLUS "R" US catalog!

THE BATTLE-READY paraphernalia had all arrived on his doorstep the day before in a huge corrugated cardboard carton printed up to look like a sandbag bunker. Thrunson, with a candy cigarette dangling jauntily from the corner of his mouth, stayed up well into the night fondling all his new gadgets and gizmos lost in a string of pathetic fantasies involving jungle tribes, night parachute jumps, and dingy hotel lobbies adorned with potted palms and slow-turning ceiling fans.

AS HE LAY on the bedroom floor in his brand-new expedition-weight sleeping bag, he read the olive-drab packing slip and saw that his $14,312 order had qualified him for a SURPLUS "R" US five-percent Soldier of Adventure discount on future "resupplies"! He wept in uncontrollable joy for an hour and twenty minutes before spending a fitful night filled with dreams of heroic deadstick landings and P-40s with engine fires.

NOW HERE WAS Thrunson actually "out in the bush" and ready to face whatever Raw Nature and Dame Luck threw at him, one man alone, armed only with guts—and a helluva lot of gear. His heart soared!

AT THE EDGE of a small clearing he flopped on his side, popped the 17 mil-spec quick-release buckles on his pack, dropped his pouch-laden web belt, and then tried to stand erect. He couldn't. It had taken all afternoon to get as far as he had, so amidst the lengthening shadows, Thrunson, now with the posture of a prawn, scuttled about to establish his base camp.

A SHORT TIME later, still unable to look up, Thrunson was

surprised by the sudden downpour. He quickly pulled out an air force–issue five-mile signal mirror from one of three emergency pouches he carried, littering the ground with magnesium fire starters, coiled snares, and salt tablets. As he stared down into the impact-resistant plastic mirror, he saw for the first time the ominous gray clouds churning above him. No, things did not look good, and he immediately regretted not ordering those laminated cloud-identification cards. As soon as he got into his weatherproof camo fighting anorak with its parachute-cord drawstring hood, he would set up the "special ops" 4-KAST-R weather radio and find out just what was going on.

THRUNSON had not realized how many pockets and compartments were in that monstrous pack, so by the time he found the radio, it was pitch black, his flashlights were dead, and his hands ached from unsnapping all the quick-release buckles.

THE RAINS continued. Thrunson, exhausted and shaking from both fear and fatigue, turned on the gray impact-resistant radio. There was only a faint hiss in the pilot-approved earphones. He decided to deploy the radio's twenty-foot copper wire tactical antenna, but he was so sore that it took yet another hour. By then, too scared to eat any of the freeze-dried, hermetically sealed lifeboat rations or nibble on a piece of his high-energy Kombat Kandy, he cowered under the camo nylon fly of his all-weather one-man K-2 Sherpa Shelter. Visions of fighting off raging grizzlies with his im-

ported copy of an entrenching tool filled his head, pushing him toward hysteria. He scanned the dark with his MOON-O-CULAR, an Eastern Bloc surplus night-vision scope, at the same time desperately spinning the tuning dial on the silent weather radio.

JUST AS HE heard the phrase "sometimes severe," a lightning bolt hit the end of the antenna! Enough current to run every bug light in Biloxi surged through the radio and up into the headset, where it arced back and forth behind Thrunson's eyes, turning his head

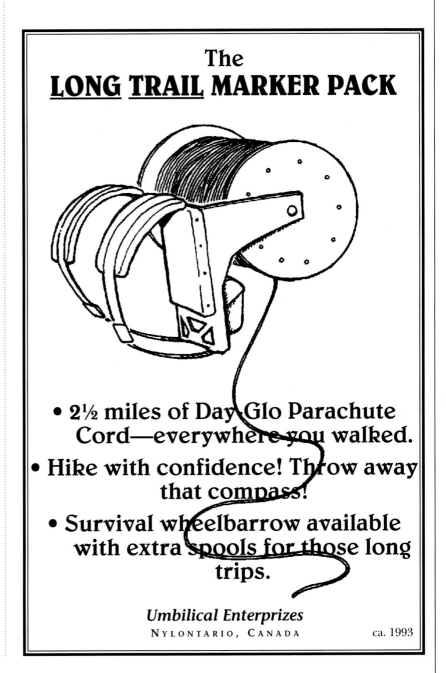

THE WIMP IN THE WOODS

into a flickering blue jack-o'-lantern and erasing forever any memory he had of high school plus six digits of his social security number. The ten-trillion candle power flash fried the night scope's delicate sensors. It lay in the wet moss where Thrunson dropped it, the mil-spec components inside crackling like popcorn. All Thrunson could see, even with his eyes clamped shut, was brilliant white, as if his face had been pressed against a Klieg light. His ears rang like he'd shared an empty Dumpster with a concussion grenade.

A SECOND strike fried the trees supporting his replica "Viet Nam era" jungle hammock, melting it into a single olive-drab filament, which, seconds later, went off like a flashbulb and was gone.

THE THIRD ONE was the worst. It screamed down from above, a dancing, thousand-forked column of blinding neon fire that hammered the remnants of Thrunson's little base camp into oblivion. The area was littered with fragments of equipment resembling pork-rind snacks bathed in St. Elmo's Fire. Each incandescent remnant made a little sound as it discharged and went out in the haze of mil-spec nylon vapor and smoldering navy-issue shark repellent. Destroyed was the Da Gama U. R. HERE satellite-fed electronic compass, the Eternex Perpetual "divemaster" alarm clock (capable of functioning at the bottom of the Mariannas Trench!), the wraparound special-ops sunglasses (will stop a 20mm anti-aircraft round!), the replica dog tags, the Septic Sipper Water Purification straw, plus eighty-one other titanium, ballistic nylon, waterproof, crush-resistant, "issue" items that had made Thrunson feel so safe outdoors. Yes, it was all ruined, except for the thirty-six-inch hollow-handled survival machete, although the blade was curled up on itself like a party horn and the needle of its secret G.I.-style compass had been spot-welded in place.

THE STORM PASSED as the last of the Coast Guard–approved T7-G31T Super Nova flares cooked off in the embers of Thrunson's pack. Overwhelmed with a sense of helplessness, he pulled the hood of his now electronically bleached fighting anorak over his head and covered himself in the ashes of what was left of his commando-style sleeping bag. Petrified, he waited for merciful dawn while his vivid imagination created more horrific images of rampaging grizzlies from the wretched sounds of a half-dozen nearby raccoons vomiting up the last of his Kombat Kandy.

AS SOON AS it grew light, Thrunson, propelled by terror, desperately raced back down the grooved trail he had made coming in. Six minutes later he was safe in his driveway.

THE FOLLOWING week he returned to the scene and quickly gathered up every bit of the survival debris he could find and promptly sent it all back to SURPLUS "R" US in the original "bunker box." He included an indignant letter demanding a full refund because, "clearly, Gentlemen, the equipment has failed to last a lifetime!" For added effect there was a postscript warning: "Remember, I am an ex-Marine!" It was a lie. In fact, no vet had ever bought anything at SURPLUS "R" US.

THE COMPANY'S response came in a camo envelope two weeks later. There would be no refund, as the equipment "ap-

GUPPIES—YUPPIES—WANNABES

RIGHT OFF THE BOAT FROM HONG KONG COMES OUR LATEST FASHION FIND FOR FIRST-TIME FLY FISHERS!

IT'S THE <u>CHUCK F. OROFIS PRESENTATION FLY VEST</u> AND IS IT EVER LOADED WITH FEATURES!

- *Your favorite colors—teal, magenta, pink, or violet (sorry, no olive, khaki, or other unhappy colors)*
- *A nifty button-down collar available in solids or plaids to really "PLUS" the festive mood of the vest!*
- *All the pockets contain foam blocks that make the vest look like it's loaded "full of fly gear." You won't lose them, either, because each "pocket" is sewn shut!*
- *Two cute plastic replicas of "tool-like things" to hang on the vest!*
- *Your choice of two nifty nylon fleecelike patches!*
  - A. **<u>WEATHERED</u>** *is slightly "stained" and contains one small fly. Don't worry—there's no hook!*
  - B. **<u>SPARKLING</u>** *is bright, new, color-coordinated, and sprinkled with tiny mylar flecks to "catch the sun"! Sorry, no fly!*

ONLY $327 AT OROFIS.

SPECIAL!! **B**uy one Orofis Presentation Vest and get 25% off any Orofis replica fly rod and reel!

Buy two and get 30% off our "Olde English Style" creel (lifting the lid reveals a trout hologram—you'll never get "skunked")!

- *Next time you're in Arlington, Vermont, visit our showroom and the Mallard Mailbox Museum next door.*

REMEMBER: OROFIS IS VERMONT'S ONLY DISCOUNT FLY SHOP!

75

peared to have been abused." However, since Mr. Thrunson Bivalve Jones was such a valued customer, it said, SURPLUS "R" US was willing to give him a miniature replica of a Good Conduct Medal! As if that wasn't enough, they would also give him an additional 5% Amateur Mercenary discount on top of the 5% Soldier of Adventure discount which he could then use toward the purchase of a genuine Russian army–issue Gorky 7 Field Pencil Sharpener! (The 3.7 volt Zil battery that powered it was no longer available; however, "troopers" were advised to order its equivalent: twenty-five D cells.) Counting freight charges on the 90-lb. pig-iron grinder, he would only be out $412.92!

IN HIS BEDROOM that night Thrunson weighed the pros and cons of the offer, as he lay in his regulation army cot, an olive-drab blanket marked U.S. tucked up under his chin. That Gorky 7 sure sounded good, and he really liked the idea of a medal. . . .

AT NINE O'CLOCK the microchip in his submarine-style night light softly beeped out "Taps," but Thrunson Bivalve Jones was already fast asleep and far away, running just ahead of the bulls in Pamploma.

THE "LOST" AUDUBONS

By Dellwoon Van Anchovy III
(*Hook & Bullet* Arts and Leisure Editor)

Art lovers of the world let out a collective "Bravo!" with this extraordinary news: Several missing paintings by John J. Audubon have been found! It turns out they were in Forton "Grandpap" Wheet's attic all along. . . .

COMMON HOOP SNAKE
Generally regarded as the world's smartest reptile, this venomous snake struck terror in the hearts of early pioneers who were traveling through the foothills of the Rockies. Achieving forward motion by grasping their tails in their mouths and rolling across the countryside, groups of the coasting copperheads often passed alongside wagon trains only to lie in ambush up ahead. Hurtling down from vantage points above the weary travelers, the revolving vipers would carefully steer themselves over a small rock or

hummock, whereupon they would be flung skyward in an arc of doom, landing with fangs bared on their hapless prey. To defend themselves, the resourceful settlers invented the covered wagon.

TROUT (CANDY CARP)

In the early 1800s this common fish thrived in waters below the dozens of candy factories located on streams throughout New England. Since workers routinely dumped the day's scraps directly into the streams, the fish grew accustomed to a rich diet of maple sugar products, quickly showing a marked preference for marshmallows, otherwise known as Battenkill bonbons. In fact, the name rainbow trout actually refers to all the different colors of marshmallows this fish will hit. Anglers were quick to develop deer-hair flies designed to "match the scraps." Called Mallow Muddlers, they came in a large variety of pastel colors. The general rule of thumb was:

"When ye water's high, give white a try; when ye water's low, 'tis pink ye'll show."

NO-LONGER-BALD EAGLE

Perhaps even more astounding than a chameleon's ability to change color is the middle-aged bald eagle's ability to suddenly appear young and vibrant in order to once again attract the female of the species. Perched atop rocky ledges, the desperate males pluck out dozens of their dark-brown tail feathers and use their beaks and talons to fashion them into a rudimentary thatch. The feather fooler is then repeatedly tossed into the air until it lands squarely on the bird's head, thereby creating the illusion of bygone days when its head was covered with healthy, lustrous feathers. Because the deceptive dome doilies invariably come off when the magnificent creatures dive for fish, they must return to their roost

and repeat the process again and again until there are no tail feathers left. In the end they are rendered unable to fly by their uncontrollable need to look young. (The name bald eagle is actually derived from Old English—ye baldy gull.)

DEER MOUSE

This animal, once North America's smallest antlered game, presented a unique challenge to dedicated hunters of yesteryear. Tracking them was tedious. An experienced woodsman

ODOCOILEUS TEENCHY

could follow them in snow—if the light was just right—but the tracks were easily obliterated by feeding sparrows. Hours spent searching the woods for rubs and signs of hooking required knees of steel. The use of tree stands was impractical, as the quarry was nearly impossible to see from any height and, due to the creature's diminutive stature, it always looked up. The only alternative was to hunt it from pits.

Taxidermists loathed them. In 1860, Ralph "Trapper" Townsend wrote, "Even with a 10-point buck (eastern count) your eyes give out in a couple of hours. And just one cup of coffee can jangle your nerves enough to ruin a mount. It just ain't worth it when all you end up with is a toothbrush holder."

REALLY BIG HORN SHEEP

Surely no other animal ever required as much patience to hunt as did this one, for no other animal ever spent as much time hidden among rocks and boulders lying prone. The great sheep could only stand up and look around for a minute or two each day before lying down to rest its neck. Nevertheless, a constant stream of rugged individuals braved hardship and mind-numbing boredom for a chance to bring home the world's widest trophy. Their attentions often centered on Montana, where the biggest herd of really big Really Big Horn Sheep rested between the Big Really Big Horn River and the Little Really Big Horn River, both of which forked off of the Little Big Horn River but are now dry. Today, few remember that

Custer's final mission was a vain attempt to capture a specimen for the Seventh Cavalry Petting Zoo at Bozeman.

TRUE WOOD DUCK

One hundred years ago startled Maine loggers marked the passage of another year in the north woods as they watched great flocks of these birds suddenly lift off the water to begin their long flight south. Yes, once again the perfectly camouflaged birds had fooled the loggers by spending the entire season bobbing about with the chips and scraps of the sawmills, totally unnoticed. Adapting to the impact of all the logging operations, the ducks had quickly evolved a pattern and shape suggesting floating debris. In a further display of nature's dazzling flexibility, they had even begun to build nests resembling small piles of sawdust.

The True Wood Duck, or Timber Teal, as it was sometimes called, is believed to be the only bird to benefit from clear-cutting. It also has the distinction of being the original inspiration for wooden duck decoys. Later, a few hunters tried refinishing their old decoys in color on the off chance they might fool the occasional mallard.

Nimrod Nevermiss and His Wonder Lab Bunky!

By W. Philpot Septus

The night before Opening Day of duck season, I always have the same dream. In that sweet reverie, I'm transported back in time to the golden age of waterfowling, to a wondrous place of blazing dawns and flights of ten thousand ducks that come to my vast set of decoys with but a single note from my call. A fine retriever sits beside me, trembling in eager anticipation. I rise, the shotgun flows to my shoulder, and I squeeze the trigger, certain that I shall not fail, because in my glorious dream I am Nimrod Nevermiss, with his Wonder Lab Bunky!

I LOVE that dream.

I HAD IT again this year, and the first duck I shot rang like a propane tank hit with a five iron. It was my alarm clock! Opening Day was here!

MOMENTS LATER, I roared out of the driveway in my hunting car, "Hatari," a twenty-year-old four-door sedan covered with duck decals and zebra stripes that I'd painted myself using a broom and a plastic wading pool full of white enamel. It was a glorious effect marred only by the grisly evidence of a grasshopper swarm that I'd driven through before the paint was dry. An aluminum lawn chair was bolted on the hood, an embellishment inspired by a movie showing a similar device used in the capture of rhino. I had ridden in the chair only once (but I left it bolted on for the "serious hunter" look). My wife, Raylene, had driven "Hatari" with the twins, Claymore and Cosmolina, along as observers. Less than a block from our house my "rhino snare," an eight-foot piece of conduit with a clothesline loop taped to the end, was viciously smacked from my hands by the stop sign we ran. At the time, all the frantic gestures of my stinging hands were misinterpreted, and Raylene continued to accelerate. Once we got on the freeway, sheer terror and the eighty-five–mile-an-hour wind in my face caused tears to stream from my eyes as if they were bloodshot showerheads. Raylene turned on the wipers and floored it. I passed out from dehydration.

NOW, AS I careened through the predawn darkness of Opening Day in a lightning-punctuated downpour, the lawn chair's woven nylon seat whistled and whined, blending eerily with the howl from our family dog, Scruffy, who trembled on the floorboards behind me. The nervous fifteen-pound hamster-on-steroids had never left the kitchen in nine years—to do *anything*. This duck-hunting trip would be a new experience for him. I was sure he'd love it.

THINKING ONLY OF ducks and glory and awash in adrenalin, I shoveled down breakfast, a half-dozen greased loops of partially cooked spackle Raylene calls homemade doughnuts. Every mile or so I'd flush my throat with scalding swigs of her "brewed" coffee, a searing mountain-grown mucilage that sloshed menacingly between my legs in the traveler's mug I'd made by laying a decoy anchor in a #2 can.

SOON TORRENTIAL RAINS fell with paint-stripping ferocity, then turned to hailstones the size of deer slugs. They ricocheted off the asphalt, taking out three of "Hatari's" four headlights and both turn indicators! In no time the windshield was rendered opaque by a thousand conical fractures; then the rear window shattered and fell in on the backseat. At that point, Scruffy was sounding like an ocarina in a wind tunnel so I cranked up the volume on my Orlando Pintail instructional tape, "Calling All Ducks!" I didn't slow down.

THE GLISTENING blacktop was quickly buried under six inches of hail, icy ball bearings that in an emergency gave us the same likelihood of stopping as a hot flat iron skimmed across a hockey rink. Nevertheless, an hour later we arrived at our destination, Abscess Pond, a tire-lined two-acre sinkhole surrounded by a wall of grotesque reeds that appeared to have thrived on whatever was leaking from the rusting reef of fifty-gallon drums at its center. Wind shrieked through the power lines overhead while Scruffy, whose pathetic voice had given out miles ago, stared straight ahead, hissing like a cobra. I was ecstatic—no one else was there!

THE HAIL STOPPED, and we emerged from "Hatari" into the industrial gray light of dawn to discover that the entire car and the johnboat lashed to its roof now had the dimpled texture of an egg carton. It didn't matter; we were there to hunt ducks. In five minutes we were on the water.

QUICKLY I PUT out the decoys, two hand-carved loons that I'd unscrewed from the base of our end-table lamps the night before. Raylene would be upset, but they looked magnificent as they bobbed in the iridescent sheen covering the pond's surface. I crossed my fingers and thought about my dream.

SCRUFFY HAD BEEN reluctant to stay in the boat but seemed to be settling down. I was about to take my knee off his neck when I heard it. A duck. It was a duck! I jammed my lucky call in my mouth and started to blow when Scruffy twisted and buried his finishing-nail teeth into my calf! I gasped in pain so hard that I sucked the entire walnut call into my mouth, wedging it irretrievably between my jaws. My lungs burned for air, as I staggered about the lurching boat emitting unearthly squawks and honks with every wrenching heave of my chest.

THEN I SAW the mallard! Frantic, I swung the shotgun to my shoulder, took up slack on the trigger, and slipped on the last of the homemade doughnuts!

MAKING A POINT

★ ★ ★

A recently concluded $45,000,000 government study has found that one dozen fish hooks and twenty-five feet of fishing line were affordable to **ANYONE** during the Great Depression! A final review panel has concluded that those individuals claiming to have been so poor that they "learned to fish with a piece of string and a bent safety pin" are "liars, idiots, or both"! So save your pity. . . .

Spinning wildly, I fell forward, ramming both barrels down into my open thermos, where they were held fast by Raylene's caffeine-laden tar. The curious mallard made a low, tight circle overhead. I reeled backward, waved the gun skyward, and jerked the trigger! Thanks to my own gunsmithing, both barrels fired simultaneously, blowing the stainless steel thermos toward heaven. Eighty feet above the water, it hit a high-tension insulator the size of a trash can, disintegrating it in a shower of sparks reminiscent of an exploding hibachi. Flat on my back, I watched in horror as the duck flew off unscathed, and a severed wire sagged and then slowly fell into Abscess Pond, releasing voltage measured in numbers normally associated with the national debt.

THE JOHNBOAT vaporized in a blinding flash of white light, blasting the duck call from my mouth and violently hurling Scruffy and me through the air in twin parabolic arcs of blue smoke that terminated in the sodden vegetation beside the car. Scruffy was hairless, and I was naked and covered with the worst sunburn I've ever had. I don't remember much after that, but I'm told repair crews from the power company, New England Radiation, found us both whimpering inside "Hatari" with a mound of soothing hailstones piled up to our necks.

SINCE THAT EXPERIENCE, Scruffy hasn't left the kitchen. Stubble-covered, he sits in the corner suspiciously eyeing the wall outlets. As for me—I'm grateful to be alive because I've lived part of my dream—after so many years, I'd finally called in a duck!

BASSIN' FOR BUCKS

If you think bass fishing has gone as far as it can go, just wait till you get a look at the Team Machine!

By Duane Snetch

An exciting new dimension has been added to tournament fishing with the creation of Simultaneous Team Bass Fishing (STBF), a unique concept whereby an entire bass team competes from just one boat. The idea dates back to the early 1960s when pioneers of the sport in central Florida hit the lakes in 20-foot johnboats powered by three outboards, with a half-dozen aluminum chairs bolted in place so that all their fishin' buddies could be with them.

TODAY'S GLAMOROUS team fishing machines are a far cry from those early efforts, however. Sporting massive custom-built engines, hydrofoil systems, and fourteen sets of temp gauges, pH meters, and fish finders, these high-performance, super-sophisticated team boats are the last word in hi-tech gear. They are also very expensive: the metal flake finish alone on Team Biloxi's "Bass Transit System" shown above costs more than two fully outfitted ordinary, old-style tournament bass rigs!

ACCORDING TO STBF rules, each team consists of fourteen members. During actual competition the team captain is responsible for everything from piloting the craft in search of

potential tourney-winning hotspots to determining when the team gets such things as rest stops or lunch breaks. Once on location, the captain must ensure orderly fishing by using a P.A. system to announce relevant information and order the type of lure he wants the team to use. For example, he might say, "Men, we're over rock structure, 10 feet, get out a jig-and-eel." Each individual team member (with the exception of the designated net man, who is not allowed to fish) then has 20 seconds to choose a jig-and-eel and rig up before the captain booms out, "Stand by to cast—CAST!" With that command the air is filled with jigs and eels simultaneously cast by the uniformed anglers. When they finish the retrieve, they wait for the next command to cast. Such orchestration is essential to avoid dangerous, time-consuming mega-tangles involving the entire fourteen-man team. Any break in the synchronized casting could cost a team victory. Once the captain decides that an area has been played out, he gives the order, "Crank in! Crank in! Stand by to move out!" With that, each angler secures his gear, swings his chair to a forward-facing position, dons his goggles, and inserts his protective earplugs. Seconds later the team is hurtling toward the next "honey hole" at speeds approaching 130 mph. As the eager competitors streak across the water riding 11 tons of metal-flaked fiberglass glory, the air is torn by the sounds of monster turbocharged engines and the slosh of a 2,700-gallon livewell, and onlookers gape in amazement at the state of the art of hawk hawlin', 1990s style.

MATCHING THE SNACK

What do stoneflies matter when you've got inspiration, mole belly hair, and No. 48 hooks?

By Bob "Livebait" Renfroe

One rainy afternoon a few years ago, I was absorbed in a wonderful leather-bound tome from the 1930s on the subject of fly fishing for trout while I mindlessly ate one peanut after another from a 20-pound can. A few hours later, I was pacing my den trying to figure out at exactly what time the pleasure of munching on the peanuts had been replaced by the pain that comes from chewing 5 pounds of salt, when I was overwhelmed by a flash of genius. Doc Herman had always said there was a correlation between my weight and my constant snacking—what if trout got large by snacking, too? For a trout, a stream is just a submerged smorgasbord, a wet food parade of minnows and mayflies. But what about *hors d'oeuvres*? What is a trout's

peanut? If I could determine that and tie a fly to duplicate it, then obviously every fish I caught using that fly would be large! My theory was flawless—I'd match the snack!

I DECIDED TO approach the problem scientifically: I'd start with the smallest thing I could imagine trout eating, then work my way up. I began with midge eggs.

THE ONLY PROBLEM was that at one-tenth of the size of a BB, a good midge-egg imitation was a bit tricky to tie. I used No. 48 titanium wire hooks custom made for me by a Swiss watch manufacturer at $40 apiece. (And I had to order a 10-pound lot to get that price!) I created the egg with a tiny pinch of mole belly hair delicately trimmed to shape. Typical midge-egg markings (black dots and pink splotches) I carefully applied using an eye surgeon's syringe and some fabric dye.

EVENTUALLY I WAS able to significantly reduce the time involved in tying each egg by using a 300X microscope. My production soared from one completed fly every three days to up to four in a single week! The microscope also came in handy when affixing a

midge-egg fly to a tippet, which I eventually began doing at home the night before going fishing. On more than one occasion I'd spent an entire day standing in a stream, still within sight of my car, desperately trying to get a wisp of nylon through that little hole in the hook. In fact, at sunset on one trip I discovered that I wasn't even holding a fly and probably hadn't been for hours.

FISHING WITH the midge eggs was dicey because they were somewhat difficult to see beyond 5 feet. Other fishermen who watched me thought I was just striking at random (which was usually the case), and several cautiously asked me if I needed help. Then there were all those cloudless summer days with the sun ricocheting off the dancing water in front of me, making my eyes feel as if I'd been staring into a wind tunnel full of sand. Usually those midge-egging days left me exhausted and hunched over with my chin creating a little wake in the water and my face so wracked with cramps from the incessant hours of squinting that clear speech was impossible. Most times I had to be driven home because my pupils had become smaller than the eyes on the midge-egg hooks.

OH, IT'S TRUE I haven't caught anything yet, but so what? I have to give my theory a fair chance; it's only been three years. How else will I know if a midge egg is a trout's peanut? Tie them and try them yourself for both science and the sport we love. And let me know if you catch anything.

A REASON TO FEAR

It's senseless to remain where you are if you smell danger afield.

—◦—⊨≡⊨—◦—

By Acton Johns

There are things out there in the gloom beyond the campfire that will get you. They are evil demons of darkness that can only be the devil's pets, waiting for you. Such creatures can do things to a man that will make him forget about life in the bush and the thrill of the hunt.

PROFESSIONAL HUNTERS on six continents regard me as fearless, yet these vile beasts of the night cause me to glance over my shoulder, once more, toward that sound in the shadows—just in case.

DO I SPEAK of the African leopard, the silent Amazonian anaconda, or even those mythic magnum monkeys of the moonlight called Sasquatch? No, there is but one species that gives me pause. It is *Ursus omigodus*, the Giant Grizzly Skunk, a wretched 1,700-pound hybrid of the West, capable of rendering a small valley unfit for habitation.

THOUGH THESE BEASTS are carnivorous and of sinister disposition, it is neither their fierce, fang-congested maws nor their scythelike claws that cause heart-cramping terror in travelers of the wild. Rather, it is their scent glands—organs weighing a mere ¼ ounce in a typical skunk, enlarged in these mixed-breed nightmares to the size of melons.

ACCOUNTS OF confrontations with Grizzly Skunks are numerous; let the recounting of a few such tales keep you vigilant!

• In the 1860s there was the ill-fated Dunson Party, innocent settlers whose wagon train was set upon by a marauding herd of the malodorous mammals. The wagon master's diary vividly describes a villainous aroma so severe that "everyone lost their appetite and never got it back."

HIS FINAL ENTRY NOTES, with bitterness, that the animals' characteristic victory yelp "still mocks our misery from the hillsides where they lie snickering like hyenas." The brave souls remain immortalized in what is now known as Dunson Pass, Colorado.

• The *Phoenix Sage*, dated September 20, 1891, tells of a hunter seeing a mule deer buck sprayed by one such odorous ogre. The muley immediately shed his antlers before slinking off down the valley. Clearly, he knew that he would not be mating that year.

• Newsreel footage from the 1930s shows Stinkin' Dan, the Mountain Man, who had been attacked six years earlier while on a survey team near Helena, Montana. Forced by the citizenry to remain in the woods, he stands before the camera, a clothespin on his nose, clad in a loincloth fashioned from the remnants of his plaid wool shirt.

TEARFULLY, HE describes his futile struggle to save his sinuses—a Herculean effort thwarted when the striped demon used its powerful limbs to pin the terrified man's arms to his sides. The ordeal is further described in his poignant autobiography, *Uncommon Scents*.

OVER THE YEARS, I have actually witnessed this vile creature's malice. I watched in horror as a good coon dog was ruined by a single spritz from a Grizzly Skunk. The dog's olfactory senses were destroyed. Today, the dog wouldn't be able to smell an open 50-gallon drum of boiled cabbage in a phone booth.

ON ANOTHER occasion I saw a petrified angler sprayed while on the shores of the Green

A Reason to Fear

A REASON TO FEAR
(continued)

River. His reel became a spool of goo, his bamboo rod delaminated, and his waders fell apart, oozing into a flat slab of rubber like a floor mat from a 1950s pickup. For a while I was able to keep 40 yards between us, as we screamed back and forth to each other in a desperate conversation punctuated by my darting about, in an effort to remain upwind from him in an ever-shifting breeze. Alas, circumstance forced me to wish him luck and leave him frantically trying to clean himself, thrashing around on the sandbar like a sparrow with a broken wing in a dusty road.

ARE WE SAFE TODAY? No, dear friend! As recently as last year, I heard of a hiker who walked into an area where two male Grizzly Skunks had fought several days before. His nylon windbreaker turned into a gray powder and blew away, along with his shoelaces, watchband, and a teal-and-magenta daypack. He was wearing 60/40 cotton/polyester-blend underwear, 40 percent of which fell out of his cuff.

SO TAKE HEED, my friend: When you are in the great outdoors, you must be vigilant, ever on guard against these vicious animals and their shimmering clouds of fetid perfume. And, believe me, I'm not telling you this just to keep you away from the places where I like to hunt and fish in peace.

HISTORIC LOONY LURES

Just when you thought it was safe to say you'd seen every goodie Grandpa's tacklebox had to offer . . .

By Dorset Vent

Here are five of the most bizarre baits ever invented. But, will they catch fish, you say. Who cares?

FRED'S FOOLPROOF FROG FLOAT, CA. 1929

FRED FEAGLE'S CRAWLER EMPORIUM, Woodstock, Vermont

This unusual float employed a simple trigger mechanism to ignite a firecracker that was inserted down the brass sleeve in the wooden frog's mouth. The subsequent detonation alerted drowsing

of this float was recently offered as the grand prize during the 75th Annual Woodstock Dace and Cheese Festival. Its current estimated value is $2800.

DINNER BELLE, CA. 1920

CAPT'N ANDY'S BAIT CO., La Farge, Wisconsin

At 16 inches long and weighing a hefty 9½ ounces, this muskie getter is the largest buzzbait ever manufactured. It was also the first lure ever designed to appeal to a fish's ego. The feeling at the time was that nothing could please a monster muskie more than eating a steamboat. Advertisements carried the slogan, Get Your fish to The Table With A Dinner Belle.

anglers that a fish had nibbled on their nightcrawler. Once reeled in, the float was reloaded and cocked. It was then drifted out, ready for action once more. Unscrupulous poachers were known to replace the firecracker with a candle, thus enabling them to silently raid stocked farm ponds during the wee hours. The only known mint example

to help the novice reach distant fish that had not yet been spooked. Starting and hand launching this gem was a little dicey. A wave of injury claims forced the company into bankruptcy in 1938.

REDHEADED WHIPPERSNAPPER, CA. 1936

HI-OKTANE BAITS, Islamorada, Florida

This beauty was one of several gas-powered tarpon flies of the era. They were initially created

U-BOAT, CA. 1924

NEMO BASS BAITS, Groton, Connecticut

This effective eight-inch surface/diving lure proved to be

HISTORIC LOONY LURES

very popular with northern anglers for smallmouth bass. A unique feature enabled the fisherman to fill the lure with motor oil through a small valve in the conning tower. A strike opened the valve and released an oil slick, thus marking the possible location of a school. It

was sold with the phrase, U-Boat Your Bass!

THE WOBBLING FORK, CA. 1834

One of two surviving examples by Julio Buel, Whitehall, New York

While on a picnic, Julio Buel is said to have observed a fish striking a spoon that had accidentally dropped into the water. Immediately rushing home, he created an extremely effective lure by attaching a hook to a similarly sized spoon. That style of lure is still in use today. Few people outside the serious lure-collecting fraternity realize, however, that Buel also applied the same logic to knives, forks, tin plates, cups, a thermos, and several different sizes of wicker picnic baskets. None met with the same success of his original creation, the wobbling spoon, though.

REEL ANTIQUES & TACKLE TREASURES

Here, for the first time, I proudly present the gear of my grandfather, the gear of a legend, the gear I now use. In some small way, I know he'd hope that, by seeing this gear, it will somehow help you to catch more fish too. . . .

By Allen Scott

THE CATSKILL COBRA

DODSON AND SONS, Carpers Ferry, New York, ca. 1908

Rumors persist throughout the fishing tackle trade that four New England manufacturers are racing to get this old standby back on the market. Let's hope so! The practical aspect of such a device is readily apparent when one reads an old ad of the day: "Tired of playing a fine fish all over the pool for 10 minutes, only to have him throw the hook just as you attempt to net him? The obvious answer is to NET HIM SOONER! Quick as lightning, your Catskill Cobra leaps out a phenomenal 14 feet, safely capturing your catch! NO MORE LOST FISH! EVER! Remember: Let the Cobra strike, just after you do!"

TYMZUP! THE SUPER ZINGER

GILROY BROTHERS ROPE AND CABLE CO.,

Bethlehem, Pennsylvania, ca. 1931

Tired of getting a cold dinner and a cold shoulder every time they came home late from fishing, Morris and Norris Gilroy finally decided to do something about it. Knowing they needed something to remind them that the

time had come to head home, they took a tiny idea and made it into a marriage-saving big idea. The result was the TYMZUP! The Super Zinger.

ONCE AT YOUR favorite stream, you simply set the dual-function timer/clutch release for the hour you faithfully promised your wife you will start home. Then place the chrome-vanadium hook through the door handle of your car. You are now at the end of a 65-foot steel leash, free to fish to your heart's content, comforted by the knowledge that you will definitely be off the stream and back at your car at the right time. As the Gilroy Brothers say, "If you can't break the cable, you can't break the promise!"

NOTE: Have your automobile's door thoroughly inspected prior to using a TYMZUP! and be sure to set *your* handbrake.

SOPWITH SPINNER
Original pattern tied by Samuel K. Drill, Lafayette, Indiana, ca. 1914–18

Shown here is the only known mint-condition Sopwith Spin-

ner in North America, the first fly specifically designed for German brown trout. No other design before or since has been as effective on the wary trout as this pattern; hence, it is often referred to as "The Great Fly." It surely must be regarded as the high point in the long and illustrious fly-tying career of Samuel K. Drill. True, Theodore Gordon and others added greatly to the realm of fly tying, but did they ever create a fly whose performance during a false cast was so superior that the fly was studied by aircraft designers, eventually becoming the model, the test bed if you will, for a series of full-size flying machines? I fear not!

We who fish the glorious Sopwith will always remember Lafayette's S. K. Drill.

THE MANCHESTER MAELSTROM AUTO WHIPPER
CONGER BROTHERS CLOCK AND WATCH CO., Manchester, England, ca. 1910

Was there ever a year that this wonderful device was not available? The original Manchester Maelstrom, and later variations of the auto whipper design, have taken the worry out of whip finishing for generations of novice and advanced fly tyers alike. The ingenious use of a solid-brass clockwork mechanism coupled to a series of Thread Manipulator Arms allows tyers to spin a perfect whip finish in just seconds. This original specimen has a capacity of an astounding 125 flies per winding, a feat surpassed by only a few auto whippers today! One can safely say that the job cannot be done any better by hand; that's why no one even tries to anymore.

NOTE: For safety reasons, always wear goggles when using any automatic fly-tying tools.

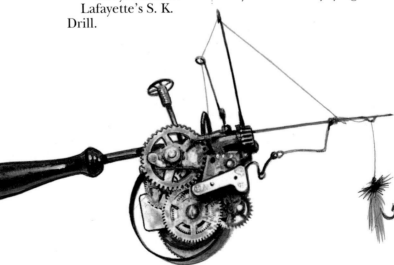

REEL ANTIQUES & TACKLE TREASURES

THE REEL TROWT CREEL ENHANCER
C.K. HUDSON AWNING CO.,
Jacksonville, Florida,
ca. 1933

Have you ever been ashamed to show your catch? Does your home state let you fish for free because everyone there knows you never catch anything? Is your fishing morale so low that you let your wife use all your fly-tying supplies to make a comforter for the dog? Has *Fur & Scales* cancelled your subscription because the angling editor didn't think you deserved it? Then go straight to the antique shops and try to find a few of these old-timers. The early Reel Trowt ads explain the solution: "BE A SUCCESSFUL FISHER-MAN! A fast glance into your creel proves to fellow anglers that 'You're in the know!' Just a peek and they see big, fat trout wriggling on a bed of ferns!"

Keep your fly rod, fella, but get some cheese or worms down on the bottom where you can catch something. Then *zip! zip!* change those dace, chubs, squawfish, and suckers into flopping, flipping, ferocious trout! Show your friends, but just for a second! 'You're in the know!'"

WHAT PRICE GLORY?

There's only one thing to do when an eight-year-old catches your fish.

By Trent Halpoon

Winter. For me it's usually a time of reflection, a time to relive the great events and experiences of another golden year in the outdoors. In the sanctuary of my den, I often nestle into my chair near the fireplace and gaze into the soothing glow of light for hours, letting the memories flood back.

NOT THIS WINTER. This winter I sat rigid and white-knuckled through the entire first week of December. I couldn't eat or sleep, and I let the fire go out. Why? I'd just found out that my eight-year-old niece had caught her first fish—not a shiner on a bread ball or a bluegill like the one I caught when I was her age. No, it was a bass. A big bass. A 12-pound 7-ounce lunker! Her family was visiting Cottonmouth World near Orlando when she took it on a plastic worm and a cane pole while "pretending" to fish in the pond behind their motel. Twelve pounds 7 ounces on a cane pole! It made the local paper, the worm manufacturer paid $2,000 for a promo picture, and a taxidermist offered to mount her trophy for *free*. (I'd had to pay extra for *my* biggest fish because the taxidermist didn't "do" carp.)

HOW COULD IT happen? She isn't even interested in fishing. I, on the other hand, spend more on bass-club dues than I spend on food. Why, I've hammered lakes all over the South for three decades, and I haven't even broken the 4-pound mark. My bass boat cost more than my first house, and it carries only a fraction of my bass gear. My wife says the only thing afloat with enough room for all my stuff is gray and has a flight deck.

BUT MY NIECE, who thinks a Solunar Table is where astronauts eat, catches a 12-pound 7-ounce bass. It's not fair. Where's *my* big bass? Where's *my* glory?

SOMETHING had to be done!

THE ANSWER CAME to me on the eighth day in my chair: I would go to Florida and fish every day until I caught the fish of my dreams—and I would take every piece of fishing gear that I own with me.

TO MAKE ROOM for it all, I am having my boat retrofitted with a TACK'L TOW'R. Built by the makers of the BASS-O-LOUNG'R reclining pedestal seat, it puts all my equipment together in one trailerable console. (It costs over $20,000, but that's no problem if I eat less and don't replace my car until I'm 106.)

IT'S GOT EVERYTHING. For starters there's a fish-identification chart right under the combination seat/lid, so I won't have that "Is it a carp or is it a bass?" mixup again. It's got a

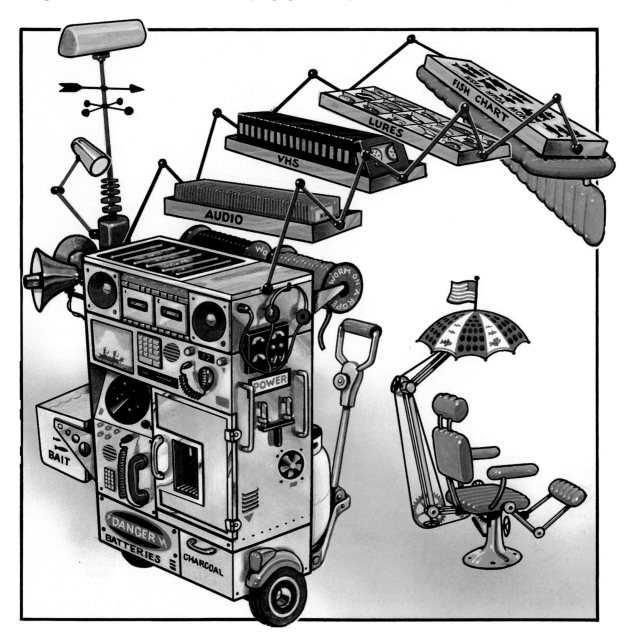

THE ULTIMATE SURVIVAL KNIFE

Contains:

- *PH Strips to check for optimum fish zone*
- *10-section fly rod, tiny fly reel, and one hand-tied midge*
- *Emergency depth-finder (spool of cord knotted every foot)*
- *6 charcoal briquettes*
- *Vial of charcoal lighter*
- *1 twenty-inch fireplace match*
- *⅓ cup popcorn*
- *4 marshmallows for nutrition and to keep everything in the handle from rattling.*

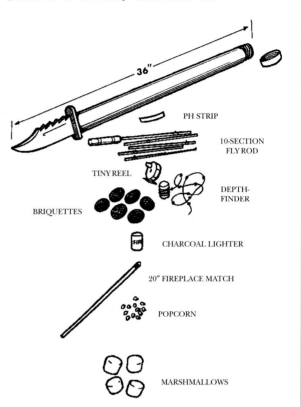

Stallone Ranger Productions
HOLLYWOOD, FLORIDA

ca. 1980

---

tray for lures, and a combination sink/livewell, so I can either store bait or freshen up. The radar (surplus from a scrapped F-4) is handy for finding the boat ramp again and for tracking other boats. There's a 1,000-watt bullhorn so I can warn other anglers away if they come near my honey hole. The weather station is another absolute necessity. I learned years ago that barometric pressure indicates a crankbait's proper speed, and the wind velocity, its proper depth.

THE COMBINATION fish finder/VHS player is part of the "psych package." If there are no fish under my boat, I can watch tapes of fish that were under Roland and Orlando's boats. There's also a boom box and a tray of inspirational tapes ("You *can* do it! A trophy *can* be yours when you free the bassman within!"). On the back of the console are spools of Worm-on-a-Rope. Instead of bringing 300 trays of worms, you just break off whatever length

crawler you need. With the hibachi and the propane-powered fridge (with a nifty thru-the-door fish-scent dispenser), I'll be able to stay out as long as supplies last. Once the trophy is landed, I can gloat to total strangers over the CB and then reach my taxidermist on the cellular phone.

SO WHAT WILL I DO with all the deck space I gain? Ha! That's where I lash the cane poles!

ATTENTION TO DETAILS

By Rodento Nucleone

I wasn't always a legend. A thousand adventures ago I was just another Joe desperately trying to get a buck with a rack that didn't look like a pair of Eagle #2s stuck in a potato. Like you, I dreamt of someday catching a trout larger than those products of Norway that come wedged in a tin. In those days I never needed a taxidermist, since my "trophies" were so small I could have pressed them in a book. Then one dismal rainy morning during deer season, everything changed. I'd been in my homemade tree stand for three miserable hours shivering so badly that flakes of enamel flipped off my teeth like flint chips knapped from an arrowhead. Worse yet, hoping it might warm me up a bit, I'd eaten all two pounds of my homemade pemmican. It was a ticking time bomb I'd accidentally crafted when, finding myself out of raisins, I had innocently substituted an item similar in appearance but larger—prunes. I had just begun to writhe and was attempting to leave my perch of pain when I slipped on the rain-greased plywood and fell from the wretched roost, shearing twigs and branches on the way down. Two feet from the forest floor my earthbound plummet stopped and I was flung violently skyward through the remaining branches in a shower of bark, pine needles, and the remnants of my lucky hat. My meteoric rise stopped when my head struck the underside of the tree stand, allowing me to freefall back through the conifer once more. The hideous activity repeated itself again and again as I rocketed up and ricocheted down. My industrial suspenders (a gift from my uncle on the fire department) were snagged on the tree stand. Those red bungee cords attached to my trousers had turned me into a flailing high-speed human yo-yo about to be rendered senseless. After what seemed an eternity I finally became familiar enough with my trajectory to twist at the last nanosecond of an ascent and grab the tree stand, where I hung upside down by my arms and legs, a wet, wimpering olive-drab sloth. I was rescued two and a half hours later by an old trapper hunting the same ridge line. The remainder of the season I spent in my den.

WHAT DID I LEARN from that season-wrecking ride? Well, I learned that an entire hunt can be ruined by something as simple as one ingredient in a batch of pemmican! It's details! Details! Details! Brother, your success depends on your attention to details! Since that day, I've never left *anything* to chance.

TAKE RIFLE SCOPES, for example. Today the average hunter never trains for looking through

ATTENTION TO DETAILS
(continued)

a scope. Well, I do! Three months prior to hunting season I begin wearing my old pair of Buckeyes-brand training glasses. The lenses are interchangeable—just insert the ones that match your scope. A 3X–9X variable simulator is also available and (of course) is guaranteed to fail when you least expect it. Most hunters leave the variable simulator set on 4X, but they've had fun paying extra. Others often practice trying to identify objects twenty feet away on 9X. Those using cheap scopes will want to train with the opaque frosted blue lenses that the company provides at no charge simply out of compassion. You see, it's the attention to details!

SHOULD THIS attitude be applied to fishing? you ask. Definitely! Brother, have you ever had a trip ruined when you accidentally slammed the car door on your favorite rod just as you got streamside? I solved that problem years ago by simply cutting six-inch sawtooth notches down the outside edge of my car doors from the top to the bottom. Now I can slam my car doors on a canoe paddle and it won't even touch it. Check with your local police before you do this, however, since the wind sucked through such a ventilated station wagon sounds like a fleet of responding highway patrol cruisers. Also keep small valuables locked in the glove compartment, since the suction created by oncoming trucks is severe enough to jerk a bowling ball through a knothole.

ONCE MORE, it's the attention to details!

WHAT IF YOU DO everything humanly possible and success still eludes you? Adjust to what you are sure to hear upon your pathetic return from the wilds by also training for failure! I recommend the "Home from the Hills" loser-friendly cassette tape, an endless loop of voices saying, "You didn't get anything? I can't believe you didn't get anything! All that money and you didn't get anything!"

"ATTENTION TO DETAILS" is my motto! In fact, I just had it engraved on my best elk rifle. Unfortunately, the fellow who did it ran out of space, so instead it reads ATTENTION TO DE-MADE IN U.S.A. I wasn't upset by it because I was prepared. I listened to a tape that kept saying, "That engraver sure ruined your rifle! I can't believe how that engraver ruined your rifle. . . ."

SPORTING CLAYS IS LOUD GOLF

What should hunters and fishermen fear most? Habitat destruction?
Hostile legislation? Well, no . . .

By Harry Trius

Something has happened to my friends, and I don't like it. For years we trailed together, true brothers of the wilderness, spiritual descendants of the mountain man and the *voyageur*. We were not "ball sport" people, engaging in the likes of squash or tennis. We were outdoorsmen who thrived far from civilization; hunters and fishermen who talked endlessly of trout and tackle, game and guns, while watching a thousand campfires die. We were hardcore.

THOSE DAYS ARE GONE! My pals have discovered Sporting Clays, and now they sound like . . . *golfers.* All they talk about are the different courses they've fired.

"HAVE YOU SHOT the Feather Hill Club yet?"

"NO, HAVE YOU shot the Briars?"

"NEXT WEEK I'm shooting at the Blue Pine Club."

THERE'S NO MORE talk of rubs and scrapes, tracks and racks; they simply drone on about the difficulty of particular stations, like bewildered duffers traumatized by a long par five. Now, the closest they get to deer hide is the trim on those cute little belt bags they wear. It's pathetic.

WHEN THEY FIRST started with Sporting Clays, all my friends made the same gushy comment, "This is the closest thing to bird hunting there is!" Pal, I didn't realize just how accurate that statement would be. Since they've discovered the damn game, Sporting Clays are as close as they've come not only to bird hunting, but to deer hunting and fly fishing as well! I'm so disappointed in them . . . all they have are feats of clay!

I USED TO think that any grown man who could talk about a putter for ten minutes without repeating himself had thrown a wheel weight a few miles back, but now I'm surrounded by friends who can orate for an hour and a half just on choke tubes!

FOLKS, GOLF AND Sporting Clays are the same (except for the decorative devices on the silly hats people insist on wearing for both). In one, you yell

SPORTING CLAYS IS LOUD GOLF

(continued)

"Fore!" and you start swearing. In the other, you yell "Pull!" and you start swearing. Much of the terminology is identical; for example, shots, swing, follow through, traps, scorecards, rounds, clubhouse, etc. It's only a matter of time before caddies lug the shotguns around and advise shooters on which chokes to use.

BOTH SPORTS originated in Great Britain, which explains why my pals have forsaken camo and are now wearing tweed. I've also detected an annoying quasi-British accent developing within the group.

"RAWTHER FINE shooting theah, Mistah Douglas" has replaced "Ya got lucky, Mooch!" One friend even pays an extra ten-spot a week to have our local gas jockey keep a straight face as he asks, "Fill 'er up, Squire?"

MY OLD PALS don't look, act, or even sound the same. They've become "ball sport" people because Sporting Clays is just loud golf. And that's not sour grapes, either. So what if my pals ridicule me because I've never broken 20? The only reason for that was cheap equipment, and the problem is solved. I secretly sold every bit of my hunting and fishing gear and ordered a top-end, full-custom Italian over/under. I can't wait to step into the box wearing my new two-tone Sporting Clays shoes (the ones with miniature shotshells for tassels) and yell, "Fore!" . . . I mean, "Pull!"

A DITCH RUNS THROUGH IT

Mile upon mile of virgin water lies waiting for anglers adventurous enough to find it.

━━◆━━

By Martin Meckal

I should have known it would be crowded that Memorial Day. Common sense should have told me that a river with pools named "Convention Center," "The Mall," and "Sea of Humanity" would get pressure. Nevertheless, I was unprepared for my first look at Vermont's famous Au Beaverware.

ELEVEN THOUSAND frantic anglers were wading, scrambling like seals on the rocks, and elbowing one another along the banks for as far as I could see. The collective motion of their waving rods resembled a limitless wheatfield brushed by the wind. The air reverberated with the piercing hiss of a thousand false casts and the crackle of shearing tippets as inept anglers popped off flies by the hundreds. A station wagon with massive speakers on its roof cruised the road next to the river, blasting the mob with its message of bargain prices at Mad Mike's Mile of Muddlers, the world's largest fly shop, located in downtown Arlington.

I WATCHED IN disbelief as a canoe flotilla of a size unrivaled since the height of the fur trade drifted out of control through the flailing gauntlet. A wave of profanity surged through the angling horde. Each craft trailed a massive web of fly lines, backing, and landing nets, while its occupants, staring wildly through a cocoon of feathers, floss, and fish hooks, desperately thrashed the surface to a foam. Rafts of lucky hats rotated slowly in the back eddies. It was a nightmare.

DESPONDENT, I climbed back in the car, ripped my trout decal off the dash, and vowed I would never fish a crowded stream again.

FOR THE NEXT two years, I methodically studied satellite photos of New England and discovered 7.6 million miles of virgin waters just waiting for the adventurous angler. It's in ditches. That's right, pal, in ditches that are teeming with minnows, a gamefish that, gram for gram, rivals any tarpon. (That is, of course, with appropriate tackle.)

USING THE SKILLS I had gained as an H-O train modeler, I built myself a splendid medium-action minnow rod of Tonkin cane that I obtained from select swizzle sticks. Waxed, heavy-duty thread made a perfect .01-weight fly line, and I fashioned the knotted leaders and tippets from baby hair.

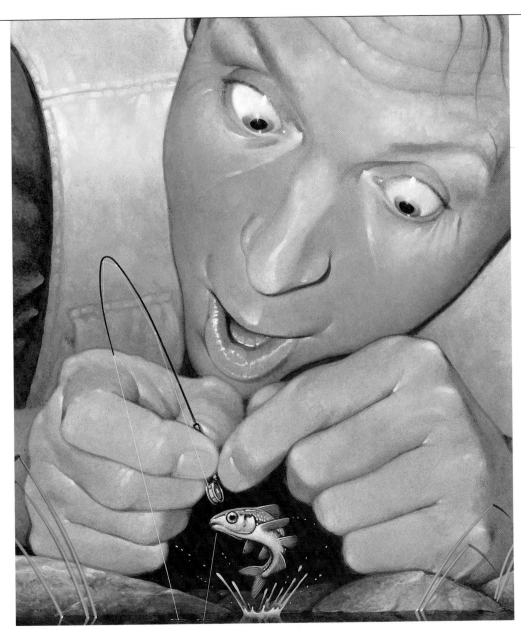

To SAVE WEIGHT, I built the reel (and a spare spool for a sinking line) from titanium. The adjustable drag is so smooth that I can slow down those heart-stopping 3-foot runs that get into the backing and make the reel scream (well, squeak, anyway).

I ORDERED A LOT of custom-made No. 48 hooks, which are ideal for my favorite dry fly pattern—the Ultra-Light Cahill. Believe me, nothing compares with the thrill of a 2-inch minnow shattering the surface when he hits one of them and then tailwalks for a foot and a half.

SURE, IT WAS a nuisance fitting ball bearings in the reel or tying blood knots in the little leaders, and yes, you still have to learn how to double haul if you want to reach the other side of the ditch. But there are no crowds, and it only costs $1.75 to get your trophy mounted. And whether it's a trout, a tarpon, a bass, or a minnow, your heart sinks just as far when the fish throws the hook. I only hope no one makes a movie about it.

LOOKING BASSACKWARDS

It took an apparition from prehistory to reveal the ancient origins of our most sophisticated sport.

By Carlton Glasshull

Two years ago this writer set the scientific world on its ear by succeeding in a quest that had cost lesser men their fortunes, their reputations, and yes, even their sanity. In a dark, fishbonelittered grotto, its limestone walls adorned with angling frescoes unseen by human eyes for ten thousand years, I found the world's oldest bass boat. It was an archaeological event equalled only by the unearthing of Tutankhamen's tomb.

MY QUEST had its origin with my reading of *Just for the Hull of It—The Search for the Original Bassboat*, by the "Anglin' Anthropologist," Orlando Mead.* As an ardent arkeologist (one who studies old boats) I was mesmerized; I felt the hardships and disappointments of the author's search through his vivid, heartwrenching description of his quest and its ultimate failure.

WHILE I WAS in the midst of my reading, a ghostly figure appeared, naked but for a scrap of fur about his waist. His unusually long arms held a primitive tackle box and a bait-casting rod spooled with 20-pound-test sinew. The apparition's deepset eyes stared into my soul, and its voice told me: "It is up to

YOU! March on where others have fallen." In that moment, I accepted the call of destiny.

MEAD'S SEARCH HAD centered on an immense labyrinth in a part of the ancient world that was a center of bass worship. Certain that the answer lay in that labyrinth, I pored for weeks over the thousands of photos in Professor Mead's book, using a jeweler's loupe to ferret out the tiniest details.

NINE WEEKS into my quest, in a photo on page 2316, I saw something extraordinary that convinced me that the boat existed. Barely visible above the spot where the hysterical Orlando beat his head on the cavern wall was a pictograph that equated a large bass with a hog!

THREE DAYS LATER I was there—Laskoal Cave in Flippin, Arkansas. In no time I found the vessel, the cause of so much human tragedy, not 100 feet from the place where Orlando's brain had suffered its final backlash.

WITH TEARS streaming down my face, I marveled at how little bass-boat design had changed since that glorious birchbark craft was built. Who could have guessed that pedestal seats were that old, and that even then, the front seat was the best? I gazed in awe upon the granite anchors, the simple knotted sinew line that served as depth finder, the short-paddle "trolling motor." There was even a livewell that was aerated by blowing through a reed. It was overwhelming!

WHAT UNKNOWN genius devised the crude wooden drivetrain lashed to the transom? I imagined our fishing forefa-

thers furiously cranking themselves across a lake to their favorite honey hole. My heart tightened, thinking of a loin-clothed craftsman using only a sliver of flint the size of a potato chip to carve a weedless prop from a 14-pound chunk of hickory. When I read the pictograph on the boat's side proclaiming, "I . . . BASS . . . MAN!" I knew I had to share this mystical experience with my fellow man.

WITH A $700,000 grant from B.A.R.G. (Bassin' Antiques Restoration Group) and matching Federal funds, I set about preserving the priceless craft for future generations.

SINCE THE DRIED-OUT bark hull was too fragile, I scrapped it, replacing it with a glass Bassin' Banshee hull from Screamer Marine. Since the new hull is magenta, I had new color-coordinated fully adjustable pedestal seats installed. They're servo-controlled, and the front one has a lumbar-massage unit.

SINCE I WANT to be cranking a reel and not some maple motor, I hung a 175-horsepower River Eater XJ from Firestorm Racing on the stern. It's loud, but I can still hear my tunes—thanks to Sound Barrier's incredible thirty-speaker system, which has the moxie to create chop 10 feet from the boat.

THE ORIGINAL RUNNING torches would never stay lit at 85 mph, so I dumped them for Super Nova halogens complete with a pair of 1,250,000-candle-power spots. You can bet *I'll* find the ramp after sunset! The knotted strings didn't look right, so now there are seventeen screens telling where I am, what I'm

over, and what the temperature and pH of all of it is.

THE NEW LIVEWELL is as big as a wading pool, temperature-controlled, and its ForceFive aerator could inflate a blimp. The whole rig's cradled down the blacktop by a fluid-suspension Hull Hugger Demon from Nemo Trailer. I got the matching bus, too. It says "I . . . BASS . . . MAN!" right on the side.

WE'LL BE AT all the major tourneys this year, so stop by. You can meet me and my driver Orlando. See ya there!

*Son of anthropologist Mavis Mead, namesake of Lake Mead, the 3-acre New Jersey salt flat where tool manufacturers test bubble levels.

NAVEL ARCHITECTURE

From one man's brush with death comes the long-awaited history of America's most ingenious device, the Delta Donut.

By Roger L. Scupper

For me, the final straw occurred July 20, 1960, about 50 miles from where Ontario's Nipigon River enters western Lake Superior. I was fishing from a homemade belly boat, working the mouth of a tiny stream for "coasters," those brawny brookies that roam the huge lake. As usual, there was plenty of action—so much, in fact, that my reel's constant screaming drowned out the whine of a rising wind. Wavelets built quickly into whitecaps and I watched in horror as the timbered shoreline steadily receded. For eleven days and 300 nautical miles I was blown eastward, unnoticed by freighters or pleasure craft, and I finally washed ashore just south of Sault Sainte Marie.

PRIOR TO THIS brush with a watery death, I had been content to float in an inner tube with just a strap to keep me from falling through the hole. But all that changed. I decided it was time I owned a stream-driven side-wheeler—a Delta Donut—like everyone else.

THE DELTA DONUT is now celebrating 110 years as the world's premier steam-powered belly boat. Three out of four serious fishermen own one, yet surprisingly few know anything about its colorful history.

THE YEAR WAS 1883 and, thanks to the Iron Horse, steamboats were rapidly losing their position as the prime movers of freight to the West. A glorious era was ending, its passing marked by the demise of the most powerful names in riverboat construction: Great Western, Steam Scows, Natchez Riverthrashers, Ltd., and the Armageddon Marine Boiler and Shrapnel Company. A single builder remained—Hellfire Steam Ferries of New Orleans. Established in 1810 by steam pioneer Robert Fulton, it was now controlled by his great-grandson (and the top bass tourney man of 1879), Orlando Fulton. In an interview which appeared that summer in the industry newsletter *Debris*, he said, "It is time for Hellfire Steam Ferries to boldly face the future! We can survive as a company only if we downsize."

TWO WEEKS LATER, Orlando Fulton fired 3,000 of the company's 3,006 employees and simultaneously reduced the scale of his company's products. Vessels once capable of bucking a 6-knot current while carrying 320 tons of cargo shrank overnight to 5-foot-long inflatable rubberized canvas novelty craft, miniatures designed to convey a partially submerged individual and perhaps tow a small cooler. Far from stately, its virtues in limited-access waters were immediately apparent to the angling fraternity, and within six months orders for just under 14,000 units had been placed.

OVER THE COMING decade sportsmen successfully employed the briquette-burning belly boats in pursuit of bass, trout, crappies, and bluegills. Then on March 8, 1895, fishing history was made in the Florida Keys when Orville "Lefty" Sprunt took the sport to a new horizon when he hooked the first tarpon on a fly from a belly boat. Unfortunately, according to onlookers, he was towed over that same horizon by the gilled Goliath; the fisherman was never seen again.

MORE CALAMITIES followed. That same year, newspapers carried reports of a jammed throttle resulting in a hapless angler's "crossing the Mississippi River near Sebula, Iowa, at a terrifying speed. The infernal machine, upon arriving at the opposite shore, proceeded to pound its way half a mile inland, dragging its unwilling occupant with it. Mercifully, its furious fires at last burned out and man and machine came to rest in a field of feed corn."

THOUGH THEIR advertising motto stressed safety ("Delta Donut—You blow *them* up, they don't blow you up!"), there was the occasional boiler rupture, in which case one of two things happened: the craft either became a violent water-borne centrifuge (a frightening effect known as "Neptune's pinwheel") or, worse yet, it became an "upriver rock-et." In the latter, the ferocious jet of steam sent the device skittering across the water's surface at speeds approached in those days only by bullets.

DESPITE THE PERIODIC accidents, sales multiplied, as did the number of competitors. The Anthracite Belle, the Glory Girdle, and the Ring O' Fire appeared briefly, only to wither in the shadow of the ubiquitous Delta Donut.

FOR THE NEXT half century the craft continued to dominate the industry. The early 1940s saw Hellfire Steam involved in the war, supplying Allied special operations groups with thousands of the machines in olive drab.

IT WAS 1958 when the one-millionth Delta Donut, still the flagship of the company, was launched, and in a nostalgic tour steamed the full length of the Mississippi River. Today it is enshrined in the corporate headquarters of Hellfire Steam Ferries. Says CEO Orlando Fulton III, "Her future looks bright. Of course, we've had to make a few changes so she can steam into the next century. She's all nylon now; we're converting her from charcoal to propane; and our engineers are perfecting an even smaller steam generator to power running lights, fish finders, and the like. They're also looking into the feasibility of a hot-water bleed-off so we can feed boiler water through warming coils in the angler's waders. Next year we'll have the calliope option available. . . ."

SO, THAT'S HER story. The Delta Donut—110 years old and still going strong!

A *CLUCKING* DISASTER

It was to be turkey hunting's finest moment. Then tragedy struck.

⊢⊣ ⊨◆⊭ ⊢⊣

By Gordon Hollister

For years, the public's perception of turkey hunting consisted of woods filled with camouflaged strangers, lurking behind stumps, trying to seduce each other with game calls. However, in 1986, two friends of mine, giants in the economically troubled aerospace industry and avid turkey hunters, made a bold attempt to change that image and, at the same time, make a fortune for their companies.

MERRIAM VON BRAUN, CEO of Stratodyne North America, and Osceola Huxley, CEO of International Robotron, enlisted the help of Sit 'n' Slash Riding Mowers Chairman H. Gould Wells, and Jules and Verne Spruntz, owners of Spruntz Brothers Game Calls. These five men formed PROJECT TURKEY 2000, a consortium dedicated to producing revolutionary products for the turkey hunter.

IN THE SUMMER OF 1987 the consortium's first offering was revealed at a spectacular press conference held in the 15,000-seat auditorium at the Spruntz Museum of Game Calls in Perdue, Tennessee. I was in the front row as Guest of Honor. Von Braun, the project leader, flanked on stage by his part-

ners, fought back tears as he delivered a moving three-hour speech in which he paid tribute to turkey hunting's glorious past, and went on to predict the coming Futurist Age of Turkey Hunting.

AFTER A STANDING OVATION, he pulled out his lucky slate call and gave the signal. The curtains were parted by two showgirls wearing 11-foot-high drumstick costumes, and the world-famous Spruntz Brothers Game Call Band tootled, squalled, and shrieked a medley of *Thus Spake Zarathustra, Ride of the Valkyries*, and "Turkey in the Straw."

HIS VOICE BREAKING, von Braun announced: "Ladies and gentlemen, turkey hunters from across this great nation will ride into the new century aboard our first product. It is the turkey-hunting vehicle of the future! I give you . . . the GOBLR*!

LASERS FLASHED and ricocheted above us, and a single spotlight shot its blue-white beam onto centerstage where the incredible machine stood. Its 200-pound cloak of nylon feathers (designed for tom foolery) had been removed, exposing a glittering vision of electromechanical glory.

IN THE COCKPIT, test hunter Orville Yeager waved to the awestruck crowd, then pushed the joystick forward. There was a soft whirring sound as the titanium turkey stepped forward to the edge of the stage and slowly bowed. Yeager gave the thumbs-up sign and said: "That's one small strut for . . ." but was drowned out as the hall erupted. Dignitaries, reporters, and cameramen fought to see the machine and scream questions at von Braun.

THE PROTOTYPE before them had been assembled from the consortium's high-tech leftovers—the warehoused scraps and remnants of past aerospace and lawn-care wizardry. The result was a marriage of glistening gadgetry from the Apollo, Gemini, and Shuttle programs, topped by a salvaged crop-duster cockpit jam-packed with controls. Between banks of screens, gauges, and readouts were buttons, knobs, switches, and bristling clusters of green and yellow levers, which at one time were spare parts for various Sit 'n' Slash mowers dating back to 1947. (The luxury vinyl seat was from a Sit 'n' Slash Turf Terror de Ville, circa 1959.)

THE GOBLR'S performance envelope was truly impressive.

A *CLUCKING* DISASTER
(continued)

Its solar-powered legs (originally developed for NASA's defunct *Lunar Leaper* vehicle) enabled it to carry a hunter at 49 mph over clear, level ground. It could slow to a trot, or creep at a stealthy 1 mph. Woodlands, fields, and rocky ground posed no obstacle, thanks to gyro stabilizers and a surplus Air Force SR 71's Landscan radar system, which was monitored by GOBLR's master computer. Terrain data was analyzed and compensated for by altering the stride of the servo-controlled hydraulic legs.

A HUNTER WOULD always know his exact location and elevation plus that of any turkey within a 1-mile radius simply by looking at a screen. The information—accurate to within a ¼ inch—was transmitted to GOBLR by the BIRDTRAX satellite system. Unused for a decade, its fifty-one satellites had originally been launched by NASA to track the return of the swallows to San Juan Capistrano.

SENSITIVE ENOUGH to differentiate between a finch and a grackle from 300 miles in space, the satellites' infrared multispectrum cameras could easily pinpoint any turkey. And once locked in on a bird, the GOBLR would sneak as close as possible and then crouch by a stump where a computer would attempt to call the bird in with chirps, clucks, and gobbles produced by an automated array of CO_2-powered Spruntz Brothers calls. Sophisticated avian audio analysis devices would interpret the turkey's response and then give the bird's height, weight, probable beard length, and projected cooking time.

GOBLR WAS TO be demonstrated the following morning at a sprawling farm where a single turkey had been hidden in 3,000 acres of alfalfa. At exactly 8 A.M., test hunter Yeager was to scramble aboard the GOBLR from a LeMans start in the barnyard, activate its systems, pinpoint the caged critter's location, and quietly maneuver the

machine to within 20 yards of it in the shortest possible time.

THE MORNING OF the test found a churning crowd of 11,214 sleepless hunters, reporters, and potential investors milling about the property. Fistfights broke out among the haggard spectators as tensions rose. Vendors worked the mob, selling coffee, doughnuts, hastily made GOBLR T-shirts, and paperback copies of Yeager's biography, *The Right Stuffing*.

AS THE TIME drew near, the crowd stilled. Then, at 7:59, a faint *cluck . . . cluck . . . cluck* was heard from a distant woodline. Something was wrong! Yeager scrambled into the cockpit and the machine came to life. The GOBLR sprinted in the direction of the sound at speeds it had never achieved before, showering the crowd with clods of farmyard muck.

AS THE GALLOPING GOBLR accelerated past the 60-mph mark, the crowd was stunned to see a similar machine burst into a distant field in an explosion of kudzu and goldenrod. Heads lowered, steel necks outstretched like battering rams, and camera-lens eyes bulging, they closed on each other at a combined speed of 145 mph, steel feet pounding, 185-dB turkey calls shredding under the pressure of wide-open CO_2 valves.

THE CROWD gasped as both hunters ejected and parachuted to earth; and then, awestruck, they saw the hopes and dreams of American turkey hunters dashed as the mechanical marvels mangled each other in a colossal clucking cat-

aclysm. The robots' confused computers, programmed to handle a 25-pound bird at most, had run amok dealing with the data of birds they had perceived as being just shy of 3 tons. Was their final destructive act a colossal cockfight or was it an attempt at mainframe mating? We'll never know, for all that remained was a mangled, smoldering heap of titanium, smashed PC boards, wire, shattered solar panels, pools of hydraulic fluid, twenty-eight wheezing game calls, and two somewhat soiled riding-mower seats.

THE MYSTERY GOBLR lookalike turned out to be a case of industrial espionage. Known as the AUTOMATOM, it had been built in secret from pirated plans by a rival consortium and smuggled to the test site, where it was to have upstaged the GOBLR by finding the live turkey first, thereby garnering the accolades . . . and the contracts.

BUT THE DREAM was over. PROJECT TURKEY 2000 was as dead as the dodo. Millions of traumatized hunters had watched the disastrous display on the national news, where it was shown again and again in slow motion with breathless narration by each network's hunting editor. No orders were ever placed, ending any hopes that volume sales would lower the unit price from $21 million to the price of a golf cart, as originally projected by von Braun.

WITHIN SIX MONTHS, both Stratodyne North America and International Robotrons went under. Their disgraced CEOs

were rendered unemployable, and made penniless by litigation. The Spruntz Brothers bought out the rival consortium and Sit 'n' Slash, where H. Gould Wells eked out a living under an alias as an apprentice blade sharpener.

MERRIAM VON BRAUN was a broken man, and spent his remaining years hanging around the Mechanical Turkey Fight display erected near the Golden Wishbone entrance to the Spruntz Brothers' theme park, "Game Call World—the loudest amusement park on earth." He passed away on Thanksgiving Day, 1992. After managing a final squeak on his lucky slate call, he uttered his last words: "Let us cross over the river, and roost under the shade of the trees."

*Giant, Outsized Birdlike Robot

DESCENT OF A MAN

What started as a return to bowhunting basics became a nightmare slide past the point of no return.

By Rex Stoop

The wilderness is the permanent repository of human folly. At once it is breeding ground, battleground, junkyard, and graveyard—a freak show with no cleanup crew.

PROVIDED NO ONE investigates, its small horrors go unnoticed. But one day while walking in the woods behind my house, I stumbled upon a diary, its pages testimony to a gruesome story.

WHAT FOLLOWS is the tragic account of a bowhunter's experiment . . . run amok.

Aug. 1, 1993
Bow season's coming up and I just realized this is my tenth year. Ten years and I haven't gotten a single buck—I haven't even seen one! Why don't I ever get the brass ring? I don't know what the damn problem is—I buy every new gadget recommended for the "serious bowhunter." I own practically everything they sell in the "World of Bows" catalogue. Nothing works. Rayleen says we could have paid off the house with what I've spent on equipment. Lord, it's depressing.

MAYBE I'M going in the wrong direction. Maybe I should forget all the super-sophisticated, high-tech, space-age paraphernalia—it hasn't helped me a bit. I bet my luck would change if I went back to the very beginning and the purest form of bowhunting there ever was; the way it was done at the dawn of man.

TALK ABOUT "serious" bowhunters. Back then they hunted just to survive, and the gear they used wasn't made out of any of that synthetic stuff, but sticks, sharp rocks, and leather.

THAT'S IT! From now on I'm going the basic route—I'll be *Ultra Primitive!*

Aug. 2, 1993
On the way to work, I stopped and piled every piece of my bowhunting gear on the side of the road. It was all there in a heap—the aluminum arrows, the stainless modular broadheads, the carbon-limbed, power-cammed machine riser bow, the fiber-optic sights, and two aircraft aluminum tree stands. When I drove home, they were gone. Rayleen is pretty angry; she says I threw away a fortune. She'll be okay in a couple of days.

YES, INDEED, this cowboy's through with space-age shaft slingers and everything that goes with them. Stopped at the used-bookstore and got a couple of old anthropology books—great pictures of ancient weapons. Stayed up half the night reading and drawing plans for all the equipment I'm going to make. I've decided to stick with a compound bow. It's the oldest design, and the reason the wheel was invented in the first place.

I'D BET ANYTHING this is the year I get my buck! I already feel different inside . . . and, only two months till Opening Day.

Aug. 3, 1993
Began scouring the neighborhood after work for outcroppings of flint and obsidian. I'm also on the lookout for yew and cedar trees for the bow, arrows, and climbing stand. This is exciting! I wish Rayleen wasn't still angry.

Aug. 12, 1993
Finding traditional materials is difficult. I'll have to substitute with what's available. Progress is slow. Hunting season is only six weeks away.

Aug. 14, 1993
My boss refused to give me time off to work on my ultra-primitive gear—so I quit. Rayleen seems really upset, but I

DESCENT OF A MAN

promised I'd get a job right after deer season.

Aug. 15, 1993
Rayleen left me today and has moved in with her sister. I don't mind—now I can concentrate. I'll smooth things over after deer season. Needed some fresh air so I took all the windows off the house this evening. Feels great!

Aug. 16, 1993
Redecorated today. Dragged all the living room furniture out in the yard and painted deer and bison all over the walls. Tonight I think I'll start sleeping on the floor.

Aug. 20, 1993
Finished lashing the climbing stand together yesterday. I

spent the afternoon carving the second cam for the bow. Only five more weeks. . . .

Aug. 22, 1993
Busy knapping arrowheads all day. The rocks Rayleen used for the garden border have worked out well. They take a good edge. Hope to start on a knife tomorrow.

Aug. 28, 1993
I worked up a real sweat today carving a sight window on the bow riser and it made me wonder what scent our ancestors used—after all, they didn't have those twenty-five-dollar bottles of Doe d'Cologne. I realized, of course, they used nothing. They didn't need to. All they ever ate was game, so that's what they smelled like. I

went straight into the basement and got a couple of steaks out of the freezer. Had them rare.

Aug. 29, 1993
I had three steaks for dinner tonight—very rare.

Aug. 31, 1993
Raw meat is pretty good. One more month till Opening Day. I sure feel lucky.

Sept. 2, 1993
My bow is finished. I'll start tuning it tomorrow. The couch will make a good backstop. I moved it next to the fence behind the garage. While I was back there, I found a real good spot to dig for grubs.

Sept. 4, 1993
The bow is awesome! I spent the morning practicing and feel very confident—I'm like a new man.

Sept. 6, 1993
I haven't bathed in a long time and my clothes are just filthy shredded rags. I don't care; it seems so natural. But now that I go outside for target practice, I'm concerned about upsetting the neighbors. I don't want any trouble so close to deer season.

Sept. 7, 1993
I tried to put on a clean shirt today and I thought the sleeves had shrunk! Something has been happening to me. When I stand upright, my knuckles are only 3 inches off the ground. . . . I'll worry about it after I get my buck.

Sept. 8, 1993
I solved yesterday's problem. I've abandoned clothes altogether, except for a loincloth that I cut out of the suede jacket Rayleen gave me.

DOES YOUR DOG MISBEHAVE?

Sept. 12, 1993
My arms are even longer. I don't know what to do. My bow doesn't fit now—I don't even have an anchor point. There's no time to make a new bunch of longer arrows.

Sept. 13, 1993
Eureka! I compensated for the change in my reach by making the bow an overdraw, and it worked! When I was gnawing on a root last night I distinctly thought I heard wolves. . . .

Sept. 20, 1993
My appearance has changed even more dramatically over the past week. My forehead is now completely horizontal and my eyebrows have merged into a single woolly strip. My eyes are beady and sunken beneath a cantilevered shelf of bone. My jaw has become a massive, tooth-congested vise powerful enough to shatter marbles. There's a coat of hair long enough to braid growing on my back. . . . I think I should see a doctor—after deer season.

Sept. 22, 1993
I was spotted gathering sunflower seeds beneath a neighbor's bird feeder. I tried to reason with him, but my speech has changed to a guttural gibberish punctuated by the clicks and rasps of my orange molars. I eluded the police by fleeing through the treetops. . . .

Sept. 23, 1993
I have moved into the cavelike sanctuary of this culvert. It is down the street from my house, but now I consider it home. My bow and arrows are here, along with my tree stand.

Sept. 28, 1993
I decorated the walls of my new dwelling with mud paintings of deer, bison, and an eagle. Soon . . . Opening Day.

Sept. 29, 1993
It is very tiresome for me to write. Words come so slowly. Don't know what it means but will worry about it after I get . . . buck.

Sept. 30, 1993
Tomorrow . . . Opening Day. . . .

November?
Long time I write last . . . Deer season bust . . . I still in culvert. . . No Rayleen . . . Walk on knuckles now—gone back too far . . . Time of big snows come . . . I cold . . . I afraid . . . Go find food. . . .

LESTERS
AMERICA'S CHEAPEST
AMMUNITION
"IT USUALLY WORKS"
LESTERS
Printed in U.S.A.

DECISIONS

What would you do if you found yourself staring down the barrel of a bad situation?

+→⊶⊷←+

By M. L. Widner

Some people view the outdoors as a place to escape from responsibility. Far from it. Hunting and fishing put us to the sternest kinds of moral and ethical tests. Here are some true-life examples. Read them, and see what you'd do.

Dilemma Number One

After a savage 45-minute fight, I had the rainbow trout of a lifetime 3 feet from the net. Then my heart constricted in horror as its thick, olive-black tail went into overdrive. In a nanosecond, my fine bamboo rod was reduced to toothpicks, and I watched the white marabou streamer leap through the air and embed itself in the T.U. patch on my fly vest.

THREE HOURS later my sobs subsided, and it was then I remembered that the fifty-year-old heirloom with which I'd thrashed the rocky shoreline had been borrowed from my best friend Bob. These were my options:

A. Slap a grizzly in the face and make the damage to the rod look like part of a mauling.
B. Start meeting new people, and make another best friend.
C. Cash in my plane ticket home and start a new life in Anchorage.
D. Return the remains with a note stating why I cannot be blamed: Sometimes one gets an unbearable itch deep in one's waders that the human hand can't satisfy.

What would you do?

Dilemma Number Two

My old duck-hunting partner Gerry brought his beautiful Lab Sunny Girl to my Welcome-Home-from-Alaska barbecue. Some weeks later, I received a terse call from him: "You better get over here right now."

MY SON CLAYMORE and I drove to his house; he met us at the front door, but didn't say a word, and I wondered why his wife Norelle was watching from the kitchen window, tears streaming down her face. Then I saw the litter. The ten pups had undershot jaws so pronounced that they might have belonged to roosting vampire bats. Lackluster eyes rolled in misshapen skulls. Propelled about their pen by abnormally short legs, the pups resembled so many yapping hovercraft. The ghastly brood's disposition was obviously that of cornered rodents.

CLAYMORE SPOKE first: "Pa, they look exactly like Old George." The awful truth was then apparent. My useless, dead-nosed, soil-the-carpet canine vandal had had his way with Sunny Girl at the barbecue. These were my options:

A. Decline to ask for a stud fee.
B. Remind Gerry that it could have been worse; Labs often have twelve pups in a litter.
C. Start a new life in Anchorage.

What would you do?

Dilemma Number Three

For six years, my friend John and I had hunted northern Maine for whitetails. In case you're not familiar with the country, it holds very few deer, but the bucks get very big. It's not uncommon to go a week or more without seeing even one, but if you do get a trophy, he'll likely be big enough to haul a load of anvils.

WE WERE AT the end of the hunt, and about to accept the fact that this mission to Maine would be as barren as all the rest. Then, on the last hour of the last afternoon, I heard a shot from where John was hunting, followed by deranged hoots and yowls.

A FEW MINUTES LATER, I found John at the edge of an old logging road not a quarter-mile from camp. He was shaking uncontrollably, his face a wild mask of disbelief, and at his feet was the biggest buck we had ever seen, heard, or thought about—a 300-pound monster with twelve massive tines. Hands trembling, I held my tape between his widest points. When it hit 30 inches, I nearly fainted.

DECISIONS

(continued)

JOHN WAS incoherent all the while we dressed the deer and broke camp. Eyes glassy, he could only repeat, over and over, "Number one in the book; number one in the book." Hours later, we had the buck trussed in a tarp and on the roof of our gear-congested 4WD. I told John that I would lash it down; in his state, he couldn't have tied his shoelaces.

WE'D BE AT home by morning, but first we had to negotiate 31 miles of logging road and 4 hours of twisting, desolate two-lane blacktop before we hit the interstate south.

I DROVE WHILE John sat unmoving, his wide-open eyes like green poker chips.

WE TRAVELED nonstop until we reached the gas station where we always tank up for the interstate. I got out, walked around the rear of the wagon, and saw that the deer was . . . gone. All that remained was the quarter-inch nylon rope, a slender white line trailing into the gloom.

I WALKED TO its end, 50 feet away, praying for a miracle, but found only a frayed wad of filthy nylon filament. The deer was irretrievably lost, and I had a problem. Should I:

A. Point out to John that he'd lost a deer, but I'd lost a perfectly good tarp.
B. Offer to spring for the coffee.
C. Start a new life in Anchorage.

What would you do?

Dear Bob,
I'm returning the fly rod I borrowed.

THE GULF DREAM

By Axel Narquin, Jr.

"Fish on! Fish on! Strike! Strike! Strike!" the mate cried out.

I SWEPT THE rod back to set the hook and jammed the rod handle into the fighting chair gimbal. The fish felt steel and was running, tearing yard after yard of line through the rod's stainless roller guides!

THEN THE SPOOL slowed and stopped. Had he broken off or just turned back toward us? Suddenly he exploded through the surface sixty yards astern! Up and up the great fish came, shuddering in slow motion. The monstrous sailfish rose and was framed by ten thousand drops of crystal confetti. Right then I knew I'd just caught the New World Record!

I FOUGHT THAT wonderful fish again and again in a recurring dream, the desperate seeds of which had been sewn when I read a travel brochure containing a vivid account of sailfishing in Florida's "stunning lapis lazuli waters." I should have been skeptical about the author's assertion, "one can almost catch them at will." I wasn't. I sensed glory, and the image of a sailfish, a big sailfish, quickly made the few New England trout I'd caught look like nothing more than colorful sardines. Having just taken up angling, I wanted a sailfish *very* badly!

THIS LATEST void in my life could only be filled from the fighting chair of a quarter-million-dollar vessel rigged with a tuna tower, radar, twin diesels, and lots of teak trim! Just like the ones in the travel brochure. Pal, I was meant to fish and fish on the grand scale. None of that party-boat business for me. Nope, I would charter a fifty-foot sport fisherman.

I SHARED my dream with Big Bev, my wife. She mentioned the cost. I told her of my need.

Again she mentioned the cost. I wheedled, I pleaded, I spoke eloquently of the personal challenge: "What if I set a new world record? There'll be product endorsements, articles, photos, books, even television! Babes, we'll actually *make* money!" Through gritted teeth she said, "I give up!"

WITH THAT ringing endorsement, I instantly became a subject worthy of Hemingway, Zane Grey, or Jack London. After only a few dozen calls to Florida, I found a charter-boat skipper and booked him! The thrill of my lifetime was scheduled for one month away, March 4, 1985. The purchase price, a paltry $925.00.

RIGOROUS PREPARATION was in order! Over the next three weeks I read everything in the outdoor magazines on sailfishing. Then I bought books about sailfishing and books about the gulfstream, saltwater fishing, and big-game fishing in gen-

eral. If a volume had a single paragraph in it concerning sailfish, I bought it. I sent for every Florida State government pamphlet published since 1940 that even mentioned the word "sailfish." I read *Old Man and the Sea*.

SOON I KNEW all there was to know about a creature that I'd only seen as a decal stuck on a camper door. For the entire week before our flight south, I labored over sports equipment catalogs, eventually learning the names of the best reels and vital information like which had stainless-steel bearings and the smoothest drags. I learned their recommended line size and what they weighed empty and full. I compared brands of monofilament and braided dacron. I even knew which swivels were best and what national angling authorities felt were the optimum leader diameters, weights, and lengths to use. I knew absolutely every damn sailfish rod, reel, hook, and line by its order number in eleven different catalogs!

I CHOSE my taxidermist.

FROM SEQUENTIAL photographs, I learned the proper method of rigging up sailfish bait, balao. I couldn't get balao alive or dead in Manhattan, so with three days left I bought a mackerel from Floaters Fish Market at 75th and 2nd to practice on. Hell, in no time I could rig up blindfolded!

THE LAST forty-eight hours before our flight, I was unable to concentrate. I daydreamed that I was standing before a huge sailfish suspended from a block and tackle. I clutched the rod that produced the miracle and in the foreground a chalkboard

proclaimed "NEW ALL-TACKLE WORLD RECORD"! I just couldn't stop thinking about it. . . .

OUR FINAL NIGHT in New York, I had a nightmare in which my leviathan began jumping, and with each jump he got larger and larger. I finally wrestled him to the boat but Curt Gowdy, wearing a yellow blazer, suddenly bobbed up right beside the glorious fish and cut the line with a pair of pruning shears! My fighting chair whirled like a lazy susan and the ocean filled with sailfish jumping as far as the eye could see! I awoke violently ill. I had no more sleep that night. . . .

THE NEXT DAY, March 3rd, we flew to Orlando, climbed into a rented car, and headed south down A1A to Stuart—"Sailfish Capital of the World"! My very first whiff of salt air was exhilarating. Its significance in my life equaled that first breath taken forty years earlier. I was winning my fight with the great fish as usual when Big Bev suddenly screamed at me. I was hunched over the steering wheel, my face only inches from the windshield. The speedometer was passing through the high eighties when I pulled my foot off the gas pedal, enabling our machine's velocity to comply with the forty-five mph speed limit.

DESPITE BIG BEV'S protests, I insisted on seeing "our boat." I had to get close to it. I wanted to touch it. Arriving in Stuart at 10:30 P.M., we went straight to the dock, where we were supposed to be at 8 o'clock the next morning. From behind a locked chain-link fence we gazed upon sixteen beautiful sportfishermen gently bobbing

at their moorings in the cool glow of security lights, their outriggers and whip antennas bristling up to the stars.

THEIR FLOWING lines were exquisite, and so sensual that the boats seemed to be alive and merely resting in a watery corral, just waiting to give an angler the experience of a lifetime. A mixture of sheer joy and gratitude for the glorious machines' existence swept over me.

I THOUGHT upon The Great Fish, now only hours away from giving himself to my dream.

"AXEL, ARE YOU all right?"

"YES, YES, my sweet, my dumpling," I reassured her, "I'm only thinking of—DESTINY!"

"WELL, IT'S almost midnight; we'd better find a motel."

IT WAS NOT until 1:15 A.M. when we finally found lodging twenty miles north of Stuart. Everything had been full, even the gas stations were closed. We would barely have enough to return to the dock.

THE MOTEL, called The Happy Clam, was a bleak cluster of eight pink stucco cottages whose decaying sign contained a rendering of a bivalve displaying a ferocious smile as it clicked its heels. Another grinning bivalve lay in bed, an orange bow in each rigid pigtail.

THE OFFICE, reeking of cigarettes and small animals, was illuminated by a filthy conchshell lamp festooned with plastic seagulls. From the gloomy corner, a "lady" with

The Gulf Dream

THE GULF DREAM

makeup caked and cracked like a fresco informed us that we had our choice of cottages, since they were all empty. "Off season," she muttered. I offered to sign in. "Don't need to. Pay in advance." As she counted the money, I asked about a wake-up call, explaining the significance the next day held. "If it's that damned important, I don't want no responsibility," was her reply. She jerked open a desk drawer and produced an alarm clock, thrusting it toward me. It was sticky.

ONCE IN OUR room I was unable to set the alarm because I'd hit my digital watch while unloading the luggage and all the cute little black numbers had gone out. I got in the car and turned on the radio. Ten minutes later a delighted disk jockey screamed, "Wowww, from the super station that never sleeps, it's 1:40 A.M.—and you're with the Night-Hawk-awk-awk-awk." I knew I could smack him easily.

BACK IN Room 13 I discovered the alarm clock's mainspring was broken. Exasperated, I sat on the bed while Big Bev undressed. The bed was little more than a padded trough with a headboard, and it put my knees ten inches higher than my backside. I rolled onto my stomach but the mattress bent farther than my spine. We solved the situation by wedging our luggage under the middle of the bed.

THAT'S WHEN I began to worry. *Good God! What if I can't fall asleep until five or six? I'll never get up in time! I might sleep through my dream! I'll lose my fish! I'll lose my $200.00 deposit!*

"DID YOU SET the alarm?" Big Bev asked in the darkness.

"YEP," I LIED. I hoped she hadn't noticed the silent clock—because I had a plan: she could sleep but I would stay awake all night. It was the only way I could be certain we would make our dockside appointment on time.

DESPITE THROBBING eyes, I lay there motionless, reviewing the Atlantic Sailfish entry in McClane's *Encyclopedia of Fishing*. Outside, an occasional truck rolled by as I went over everything I knew about *Isotiophonus platypterus* from tackle to life cycle. All the information flew through my mind in flash-card fashion. I was a living computer collating the only subject in its memory bank. I regained confidence, suddenly aware of all I'd learned in a mere thirty-three days.

SOON I BEGAN feeling sorry for all those poor souls asleep in Stuart—in the entire North American continent, for that matter, who would arise in the morning and live out a routine day. They were so unfortunate not to be me!

AS I THOUGHT of the taxidermist, I saw my great fish frozen in mid-jump and bolted to a slab of solid walnut the size of a door. On a brass plaque I would acknowledge the creature's courage with the line "A Valiant Foe."

OH GOD, victory would be so sweet, the natural extension of my life's path, and a quantum leap in my brief experience as a fisherman. Thus far my best catch had been a three-pound catfish taken from a DeKalb farm pond on a thimbleful of petrified Velveeta. I saw a trophy-crowded den and my pulse skyrocketed. . . .

IN THE DARKNESS I grinned, for the next night I would go to bed a member of "The Brotherhood." Yes, I would join angling's immortals—Lefty Kreh, Mark Sosin, Al McClane, Lee Wulff, and the most accomplished angler in all Florida, Stu Apte! I began to hum, "Why me, Lord?"

TIME DID NOT PASS, just the pain in my eyes increased and their lids fluttered uncontrollably. I began squinting. Then, an hour before dawn a thin buzzing started in my head that was not to leave for days. At last I could make out the form of our car through the rotting curtains. *Light! Oh, sweet light!* I thought. *At last the dawn of my day!*

EASING FROM BED, I dressed and slipped outside. The Nighthawk-hawk-awk-awk-awk told me it was 5:25. Another hour and twenty minutes before I could wake Big Bev. I stayed in the car.

NEW PARTS of me began to complain and that damned buzz grew louder. I didn't care, though; I'd be getting my trophy soon. I could have endured a root canal.

WE LEFT THE motel on time and stopped for breakfast at "Pancake World." There a sixty-

Coral·Cola

America's #1 Ground-Up Fish Drink!
It's SO-O-O Refreshing!

ca. 1957

THE GULF DREAM

five-year-old cheerleader created Blueberry Pancakes Deluxe by pouring thin ink over six plaster discs. We began eating the things, certain they were altering our chromosomes. Before I finished, my eyes began to water profusely and seemed to produce a "click" whenever I blinked. Tears dripped off my nose onto the cobalt breakfast. Lost in a bitter fog of exhaustion, I picked up the plastic cow's-head cream pitcher, snapped off its horns, put on my lucky sunglasses, and we left. It was 7:15 A.M.

HALF AN HOUR later we were dockside. The vessels were even more gorgeous in the morning's light, their brilliant white forms accented with chrome, stainless steel, and teak. Blue nylon ropes tethered the fiberglass beauties to black iron cleats.

WE WALKED past *Wanderlust*, *Gulf Dream Lady*, and *Blue Water Princess*. There, between *Atlantic Star* and *Miss Adventure* lay our boat, *Tunza Fun. Oh, my God*, I thought, *Vandals! Vandals painted the name of my boat on this thing. It can't be my boat!*

TUNZA FUN was floating ugly. Short, wide, and very old, it had no flowing white forms sculpted in fiberglass and teak. It was Kelly green—every inch of it! I guessed the paint had been on sale. There was no glamorous flying bridge—no stately tuna tower, just a decayed grating—and a corroded ship's wheel. A vertical windshield (from some '50s convertible!) protected the craft's pilot.

It wasn't even tinted. A small canvas awning stretched back from the top of the windshield and over the cockpit to an asymmetric arch of zinc gray plumbing pipe. *Tunza Fun*'s crude outriggers were simply two cane poles. The wooden fighting chair, which originally saw service in a 1940s office, was held in place with stove bolts. It too was green. The mental film of my great day slipped in the sprockets, my vision blurred, my chest hurt, and I realized I was very tired.

DOWN THE DOCK a piercing voice bellowed, "Les' git some fish, gawdam!" It belonged to our skipper, a ruddy-faced thick-set man in his mid-fifties, dragging a red cooler. A glum youth of fifteen followed with two large canvas bags.

"MAGLAWGLINS? Gladameecha. Jim Miller." And pointing to the boy, "Smah son, Jeeder. Say g'morn, son— s'Maglawglins." The boy tried to look thrilled, failed in the attempt, and disappeared into *Tunza Fun*. A brief discussion and we were ushered on board. "Mill," as we were ordered to call him, made some final checks, and suggested again, "Les' git some fish, gawdam!"

JEEDER STOOD by to cast off, Mill fired up *Tunza Fun*, and a cloud of blue smoke spread gently over the vessel, thoroughly neutralizing any positive effect I'd gained from abandoning cigarettes.

"RAHT FULL ruddah!" roared Mill.

"BOGIE AT seven o'clock," yelled the obscured Jeeder, and they dissolved in laughter. We were underway.

SURE I'M TIRED, I told myself, *but I'm about to join The Brotherhood. Maybe in two hours, maybe five hours, but at last thank God I'm waterborne.*

THE ST. LUCIE INLET passed slowly by, and Jeeder opened the cooler. Inside were two-dozen balao, each fully rigged and wired to a 7/0 hook. So much for my practice on a mackerel. Big Bev sat on the starboard gunwale while I shielded my eyes from the light ricocheting off our wake.

JEEDER WENT BELOW, returning with a rod and reel, and slid it absently in the port rod rest. It was 5 feet of solid fiberglass that resembled the jack handle on a logging rig. I'd never seen a rod that thick. The reel, easily the size of a coffee can, was spooled with line no thinner than coat-hanger wire. I tried to sound nonchalant. "Say Jeeder, what size line are we using? Looks like eighty pounds!"

HE NODDED in the affirmative and continued checking the bait. Eighty pounds! I'd been joking! *My God*, I thought, *Stu Apte uses twelve-pound test.* What happened to sport? I could retrieve an engine block with line that size! I mulled it over: *Hell with it. I won't tell anyone it was eighty-pound test. They don't need to know.* I closed my eyes. The pain and the infernal buzzing persisted. *Twelve-pound, eighty-pound, three-thousand-pound test—who cares! I just want my sailfish.*

WITHOUT WARNING, the gurgling roar increased and I

lurched sideways, gouging my buttock on a gunwale cleat. Mill had punched our scow full throttle as we passed the St. Lucie Breakwater. We were now churning due east toward the Gulf Stream. I read Mill's lips: "Les' git some fish. . . ."

THE SEAS WEREN'T rough, the problem was *Tunza Fun*'s hull design. Each swell smashed into the blunt bow and seemed to stop us, creating a sensation not unlike a roller-coaster punching through a series of brick walls.

CLUTCHING the corroded awning pipes, my eyes streaming uncontrollably, I realized that Jeeder was staring.

"GONNA TAKE over the boat when your dad retires?" I blurted, anxious to prove I was conscious. The voice was familiar but far, far away.

HE SEEMED to sneer but said nothing and began positioning the outriggers. *This is costing me nine hundred plus and he acts like there's no money in it?* I thought. *Damn kid's an ingrate*, I scoffed, *The hell with him!*

IT TOOK US forty-five minutes to reach the deep blue waters of the Gulf Stream. I might have dozed on the way out, I'm not sure. Vague images of that kid doing something or other are mixed with fragments of a conversation with Big Bev, her quivering voice punctuating the gurgling thunder. "I don't feel good—should I eat something or should I lie down?"

"GO LIE DOWN forward," I said, pointing at the cabin hatch. As she reeled away, we smashed through another

wave, and her yellow terrycloth hat with the embroidered sailfish blew off, landing in our wake where it rested briefly like some Martian jellyfish, then sank.

THE CORNERS of my mouth ached from the sustained squinting. It seemed everything reflected light. I consoled myself, *At least we're in the lair of the sail!* I used "sail" to be like our skipper.

WE SLOWED, *Tunza Fun*'s engine idled down to a grinding throb, and Mill and Jeeder went about setting out the bait. The balao would be thirty to forty yards behind us, the reel set so that additional line could only be pulled free by a fiercely attacking sailfish. Jeeder steadied the rod, and Mill grasped the line and clipped it to the port outrigger. The bait would travel just below the surface on the outer edge of our wake. When my sail hit, the line would pop from the clip. Then it would just be me and the fish! I could see Papa Hemingway's face in the wake. "Welcome, Son," he said. I knew I was home. . . .

I SAT IN the fighting chair as we trolled at a steady eight knots. Behind us the bait undulated sensually, inviting up from the depths the one creature that could elevate my existence! *How close is he?* I wondered. I stared toward the balao until I could no longer focus.

AN HOUR LATER I edged up to Mill. "What do you think?"

"HARD TO TELL," he answered. I returned to the chair.

MY WIFE REAPPEARED, her face an unusual shade I had not

seen before. She took a picture of me and went back in the cabin.

JEEDER SPOKE with Mill a couple of times, then sat on the cockpit deck, his back against the cabin bulkhead, and began reading a book about a dead rock star.

I WAITED faithfully in the chair with eyes raw and a strange new sensation growing in my arms, legs, and the tops of my feet. Puzzled, I pulled up the sleeve on my T-shirt and then checked above my shorts. The protected areas were white, everything else looked like Hawaiian prime rib.

I LOOKED CLOSELY and whimpered at the sight of hundreds of tiny blisters. Tired, hurting, and awash with the seventeen cups of coffee I'd forced down since breakfast, I watched as my hands fluttered spasmodically and tried not to think about my burning bladder. *I've got to be more careful*, I thought. *That sailfish will be here soon!* Big Bev moaned weakly as I entered the cabin and clawed open our duffel bag. I pulled out a long-sleeved shirt—my lucky fishing shirt. It would protect my arms. I attached our towel to the front of my shorts. It looked like a pink loincloth, but it at least offered protection for my legs. Jeeder casually tossed me a pair of socks and motioned toward my baked ankles. I declined. Twenty minutes later I was wearing not only his socks but a filthy pair of his cowhide work gloves, for by then the backs of my hands were parboiled. Sweat flowed from under my lucky 4X Stetson, making momentary black spots on the green deck paint and drying

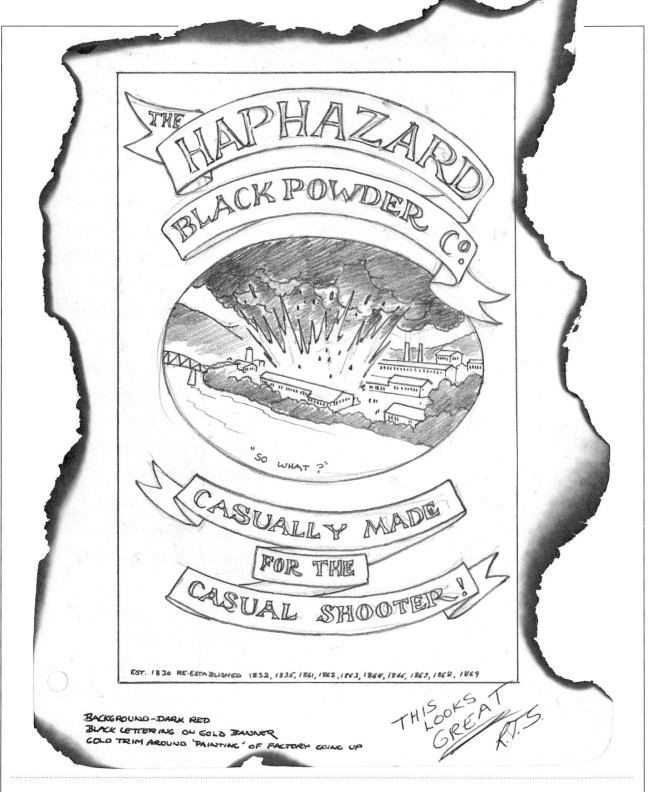

This artist's sketch (enthusiastically approved by company president Reginald T. Slippshod) is all that remains of the company. Established in 1859 and leveled in 1860, it was leveled and rebuilt repeatedly (1861, 1862, 1863, 1864, 1866, 1867, 1868, and 1869). This was to have been their first poster, however, the explosion of 1870 dashed any possibility of that.

THE GULF DREAM

there in a puff of steam. Only God knew the temperature inside my ensemble.

VALIANTLY I fought off endless thoughts of sleep and death. *McClane wouldn't doze through a world-record experience! Sosin wouldn't. Stu . . . Good God! Stu Apte wouldn't even blink!* I concentrated as best I could while all the noises continued, rising and falling—the noise in my head, the noise of the boat, and the periodic scream "Les' git some fish, Gawdam!"

WHILE I ROASTED in my anti-sunburn outfit, Jeeder waded through another chapter about the damned dead rocker. *When that sail is on,* I thought, *I've got to shed all of this crap so we can get a decent picture.* I was motionless in the fighting chair. *So much for all that tropical cocoa butter goop I put on.* Sweat, which was spraying from every pore, had washed away completely three full quarts of it. *Should have used cosmoline. . . .*

JEEDER GOT UP, snapped the line free of the outrigger clip, and began reeling in the bait. Without a word, he cut the line in front of the hook, tossed the bait to the deck, tied a fresh balao in place, and dropped it over the transom. Once it was back the requisite thirty yards, he clipped the line back to the outrigger, sat down, and worked the hook out of the old bait. The hook salvaged, he flipped the shred of useless baitfish over the side, carefully wiped his hands clean, and rejoined his departed rock star. *Tunza Fun* plowed on, its engine's decibels no doubt killing fish in our path as effectively as dynamite.

LATER, PERHAPS 2:30, I nervously asked, "Whatya think, Jeeder?" Without looking up, he made a "thumbs down."

WHAT THE HELL does he know! I thought. *Besides, my sailfish has over an hour to show up!* Looking off to the horizon, I softly wiped my eyes.

"LES' GIT SOME fish, Gawdam!" *Yeah, that's right Mill, talk that sail up here. Say some more Mill, make it work Mill, please, for God's sake, I need that sailfish!*

NOTHING HAPPENED. My throat was constricting like a kid taking a school test with four minutes left and twenty-five unanswered questions staring back at him.

WE PASSED BY Stuart several times in our circuit. Up with the Gulf Stream and down against it. Now we were below the town, traveling north.

WHERE THERE'S LIFE, there's hope, right? Right! Damn right! I said to myself. *We've got twenty whole minutes yet. If that monster hits with two minutes left, they won't cut him off, no sir! We'll be out here 'til the crack of doomsday if that's what it takes! We're heading toward him now! He's just up ahead! Waiting. Boy, when he hits, all hell's going to break loose. Any minute now.* It was a maniac's mantra of desperation that I told myself again and again. I knew absolutely in my heart, with the truest thought I'd ever had in my life, that my world-record fish would hit in the fi-

nal millisecond. Surely this would be the most dramatic catch *ever* heard of in Stuart! I believed it in my soul! Everything was going to begin in a split second. Here he comes—up from the reef, rocketing toward the barbed steel tethered to my soul! My mind was clear, my eyes sharp, my arms and legs no longer burning, the buzzing stopped. Oh God, I was ready. It would be NOW! NOWWW!

"REEL 'ER IN, Jeeder! Les' git some dinner, Gawdam!"

"THIS IS NOT happening!" I blurted. In a moment the line was in, another hook salvaged. I began falling end over end, surrounded by cross-sectional drawings of reefs, pictures of fat old men standing by enormous billfish while ads for custom rods and reels of every description swirled around me. A voice said, "Hi, I'm Stu Apte," then it laughed. The fighting chair transformed itself into a pillory—a Fools' Seat. *Fighting chair? What fight?*

WE TURNED hard west for Stuart. *Sailfish Capital of the World? Bullshit.*

I GOT UP, then tripped on the pink loincloth, and crashed down into the cabin. Big Bev was sprawled on the bunk. "Is it over, Papa Narquin?"

I COULD NOT TALK. "Look what I found," she said, slowly pushing a photo album across to me. It was black vinyl with an iridescent sailfish decal on the cover.

MECHANICALLY I opened it. Every single page displayed color photos of sailfish. They

THE GULF DREAM

were jumping, they were tail-walking, they were alongside *Tunza Fun* with a foot-long balao still in their mouths! Pictures showed them being hauled on board! Sailfish by the dozen for page after merciless page. They hung suspended from blocks and tackle. Young women stood by them beaming, holding the very same rod and reel I had used. Old men held the fish's dorsal fins up in a grand display—old men from Ohio who fished for sailfish once, just for the hell of it, and got the brass ring!

THE LAST TWO pages showed truly enormous sailfish. Not one, but eight monstrous things. They were beautiful, awesome, nothing short of magnificent—glorious tributes to the functional beauty of nature. And they were all caught by Jeeder.

I LOATHED that kid. I loathed him and his dead rock star. Who let him in The Brotherhood anyway . . . ?

I WAS BREATHING like a racehorse. "Are you okay?" asked Big Bev.

"MAYBE," I answered her.

WE SEEMED TO travel no more than fifty feet before *Tunza Fun* was tied up. The diesel was shut down, and we took our gear off, while fat bluejays squawked from the oak trees around the parking lot. I can remember handing over lots of ten-dollar bills plus a couple extra for the tip. Sure, I was still a sportsman. You bet. They had done their part. I couldn't fault them. I would have cried, but I'd long ago sweated away all available liquids. Mill said something about "not winning every race," and there was some handshaking. That was it. As we walked toward the car I felt sorrier for myself than I'd ever felt before in my life. I expected glory, there was never any doubt. I'd been alive more than 14,000 days, this was to have been the biggest—"The Day I joined The Brotherhood." Instead, I'd been up 36 hours straight and had managed only 7½ hours' sleep for the entire week. For what? What?

OLD HURTS came back, like the time I didn't make Little League and the time Irma Jean Jamison said that I looked stupid. . . .

I LEANED AGAINST our car and wiped my eyes on my sleeve. As I fumbled with the keys, I saw Jeeder walking up the dock once again looking for his place in that book.

I STILL DON'T remember crossing the parking lot or racing over the hood of that Corvette. I just remember heavy breathing and Jeeder's bewildered face as it disappeared beneath the surface. Then there were fistfuls of paperback pages everywhere—on the water, in the tropical shrubs, and swirling all about me. They floated about, sharing the humid Florida air with the only two words Jeeder said to me all day. Words that he repeated again and again as we headed north and away from Stuart—Sailfish Capital of the World.

EPILOGUE

The second day we were back in Manhattan, Big Bev came into my studio with a computer printout.

"GUESS WHAT? Counting airfare, car rental, gas, food, drink, motels, charter, tips, taxis, phone bills, fishing books, and bus fare to the library, those two balao cost you $1,893.12 a pound."

THAT WAS a year and a half ago and God, did I learn my lesson! You see, I've read even more about sailfish since then and it seems they're far more unpredictable than I thought.

THAT'S WHY this year when we go to Florida, we'll go for tarpon. Big tarpon . . . the kind Stu Apte gets.

Shortly after hooking the biggest bass of his life, Bubba Ahab was chagrined to realize he would not be needing the services of a taxidermist, but a mortician.

WITHOUT A PADDLE

By Trevor Golden

Note: The following interview with legendary canoe builder Cyrus P. Filbert was taped July 6, 1989, at the Filbert summer cottage on Little Serenity Lake, Maine. The enigmatic Mr. Filbert was questioned by T. Gaylord Gilstead, Associate Editor of *Still Waters & Quiet Craft*, the now-defunct quarterly dedicated to "achieving aura awareness and universal harmony through canoeing."

T. GAYLORD GILSTEAD: Mr. Filbert, for decades you have been revered as this century's preeminent builder of birchbark canoes. Your book *One with Nature: The Bark Canoe* (now in its thirty-seventh printing), with its wonderful blend of technical information and environmentally sensitive philosophy, is a beloved classic. To this day it continues to inform and inspire those who love the Earth and those gentle craftsmen who share your idealization of that canoe's simple elegance. Such recognition for your beautiful work must be very satisfying indeed.

CYRUS P. FILBERT: I suppose. Best thing is, all that money lets me get the hell out of Maine every winter.

TGG: Well, uh, I see. Perhaps you could tell me what your early years of canoe building meant to you?

CPF: Blackflies.

TGG: I beg your pardon?

CPF: I said blackflies! Say, where are you from?

TGG: Iowa.

CPF: Listen, Flatlander, Maine's only got two seasons—winter and blackfly! Them flying bloodsuckers can swarm in on a Northwoods bull moose and five minutes later he's been reduced to hoof prints! Any time I was ever out strippin' birch bark for a silly damn canoe, them flies was busy strippin' my hide! Who needs that? I don't!

TGG: Gosh, I'm sure that aspect of your art is a bit unpleasant, but compared to the spiritual satisfaction gained from producing a watercraft of such natural grace, such poetic symmetry . . . Indeed, the birchbark canoe is a veritable symbol of . . .

CPF: Better eat some red meat and clear your mind, fella! Them bark canoes are slow, they leak, and as soon as you finish one, they've started to rot. When you patch them with that melted spruce sap, why you smell like cheap room deodorizer for a week! The damn things only make sense in a museum or bar! In fact, that's the only reason I made my first canoe. Got commissioned to build her for the Paddle-On-Inn, over t' Skowhegan, back in '46. I use to hang out there. . . .

TGG: You built your first canoe as—as—a pub decoration?

CPF: Sure. Owner knew I was good with my hands, asked me if I could make an old-looking canoe to hang over the bar, you know, as part of the decor. Well, I done it, and like most of those early ones I made, it never got near the water. Only thing she ever carried were dead moths that kept falling out of the colored lights.

TGG: I . . . I was under the impression that in those days you were an outdoorsman, that you lived intimately and at peace with Nature, that you . . .

CPF: Why, ya' dumb flatlander, I reckon a logger is about as much of an outdoorsman as you can get!

TGG: You were a logger? Please don't tell me you cut down trees!

CPF: Only the vertical ones. How else can you clear-cut?

TGG: Oh, my God! But then you had a revelation, right? You saw the hideous ravages of logging, and that must have kindled a desire, a hunger in your soul, for a new relationship with Earth! Right? As you built that first canoe, you were overcome with a new sensitivity, a . . .

CPF: I better open a window—your brain needs air, fella. What I saw was that two weeks of bending bark paid better than two months of making stumps!

TGG: So you got started for

WITHOUT A PADDLE

purely commercial reasons? Not for the art, not for the beauty, but for . . . *the money?*

CPF: I got started 'cause of common sense! Anyway, Shakespeare, I doubt you turn down checks for writin' your articles.

TGG: I guess because of your book . . . I always assumed there was more of a spiritual aspect to it.

CPF: Of course there was! I figured my spirits would pick up right smart when I got paid. They did!

Anyway, 'tweren't long before the Chugga-Logger Bar over t' Millinocket wanted one too! Then came The Beaver Pond, Maine's first singles bar. They wanted six canoes and some paddles! My business was off and running! Three years later Filbert canoes were lending atmosphere to a hundred and fifty bars all over Maine, New Hampshire, and Vermont! 'Bout that time, orders also started coming in from a few high-roller traditionalists who actually wanted to use them! The twits spent half their time bailing and half their time patching, but that was alright. They were happy in their little world, pretending to be voyagers. Right quickly, I started hiring fellas to get the bark, spruce roots, and the rest of it for me, while I worked in my garage. Never saw one black fly the whole time, and I was making more dough than a bakery! Yup! That was damn good money in 1950! Bought my first powerboat that year, *Screamin' Mimi.* Lord, she could fly!

TGG: Mr. Filbert . . . I'm just . . . stunned!

CPF: I know what you mean—most people wouldn't think there was that kind of money in it. It gets better! The curator for the Boston Museum of Revolu-

tionary War Debris saw a canoe of mine while he was on vacation. One thing led to another, and before you know it, I was making "old-looking" bark canoes for museums all over the U.S. and Canada! Had a whole range of birch styles, some wood and canvas, too! Soon I had a full shop with nineteen workers and two secretaries churning them out. We used the scrap to branch over into crummy "old-looking" snowshoes and cross-country skies. Sold thousands of them to antique dealers all over New England! Motels, lodges, and restaurants snatched up the rest. They love to bolt that stuff all over their walls. Yessir, the whole canoe thing's been like printing money! 'Course, the company's much bigger now, what with the cute outfitter shops and the rest of it.

TGG: Mr. Filbert, you sound so totally different from the inspirational man in the book you wrote. I'm sorry, but I just can't understand . . .

CPF: That book? Hell, I never wrote that book. We put it out years ago as sort of a promotion gimmick for my first outfitters store. It was all made up. You know, "the everlasting words of wisdom from the old man of the woods" slant. Hired a girl to ghostwrite it for me—an English major up from the State college named Maude Wharton. She was working that summer as a waitress in a bar over t' Moosehead Lake. I met her while I was delivering their canoe. Yessir, that was 1953, and we've been splitting the royalty checks ever since. Today she manages the country's largest string of jet-ski rentals.

TGG: You didn't even write the

WITHOUT A PADDLE

book? All you do is pay people to build your canoes? You never ever believed in the purity of the simple life, did you?

CPF: I never believed in boredom! I wanted options—excitement. Listen, before you choke on your granola, why don't we take out Jezebel?

TGG: Jezebel? Is she your wife?

CPF: Nope. She's twenty-four feet of Kevlar, graphite, and aluminum poked down the pond by nigh-on four hundred horses! When I pour the coal to her, that stainless screw gets her up like a hydroplane—sixty, maybe seventy miles per hour. With that milled titanium bow you don't have to worry about hitting anything either—she can split an anvil. 'Course, she does sound like a P-51! Reckon the noise echoes down the valley some, 'cause early mornings I take her out when it's calm and you can watch all the lights come on at the end of the lake, damn near five miles away! Idiots used to run out and stare up at the sky. Now they just look for the exhaust flames and the rooster tail! They know it's only ol' Cyrus takin' his exercise. Heh! Now that's *my* kind of canoe!

TGG: Few people would call that a canoe, Mr. Filbert.

CPF: So what!

TGG: But the peace, the tranquility . . .

CPF: There's a lot of other lakes in Maine—they can move! Anyway, her noise don't bother me one bit. My years bucking chain

saws and racing motorcycles, stock cars, and snowmobiles fixed it so's I couldn't hear dynamite if you set if off in my oatmeal. . . .

SAY FELLA, why are your eyes watering?

TGG: Well . . . I had such expectations. I had the impression you were sort of a saint, you know . . . a modern Thoreau.

CPF: You need your head candled. I'm seventy years old. I don't have time to waste. I want to get where I'm going, not float around straddling some handmade bucket of bark, fighting headwinds with just a glorified spatula. Besides, I did it a long time ago—once. I've always liked to move . . . and move fast!

NOW BLOW YOUR silly nose and let's take a spin around the lake. Come on, you might like it! Bring your camera—there's some nesting loons. You could get pictures!

TGG: Loons?

CPF: Yup!

TGG: I don't know . . . [sniff] . . . can you get close?

CPF: Close, why I'll get us close! Probably see a moose, too! They don't like Jezebel at all—so they usually charge her! You could get some mighty great action shots, sonny. Wouldn't your magazine like that?

TGG: They'd pay extra . . .

CPF: Much extra?

TGG: Quite a bit.

CPF: Well, flatlander?

TGG: . . . I'll need a lifevest.

SHORTLY AFTER THIS interview, Mr. T. Gaylord Gilstead resigned from *Still Water & Quiet Craft*, sold all his sandals, and began eating steaks again. In 1991, he wrote the national bestseller: *YOU CAN'T HUNT TOFU and Other Drawbacks of Vegetarianism*. The following year, Mr. Gilstead and Mr. Filbert formed Oil-on-the-Water Press and began publishing the highly successful motor canoe journal, *Throb*. That summer, their entry, *Screamin' Mimi II*, took the Unlimited Class honors at the Power Canoe Internationals, in Lake Louise, Alberta. Their coffee-table book, *WET THUNDER: Power Canoeing America's Wilderness*, scheduled for Christmas of 1995, is eagerly awaited. On June 6, 1994, T. Gaylord Gilstead married Erma Jean Wharton-Filbert.